CROCHET
for babies and toddlers

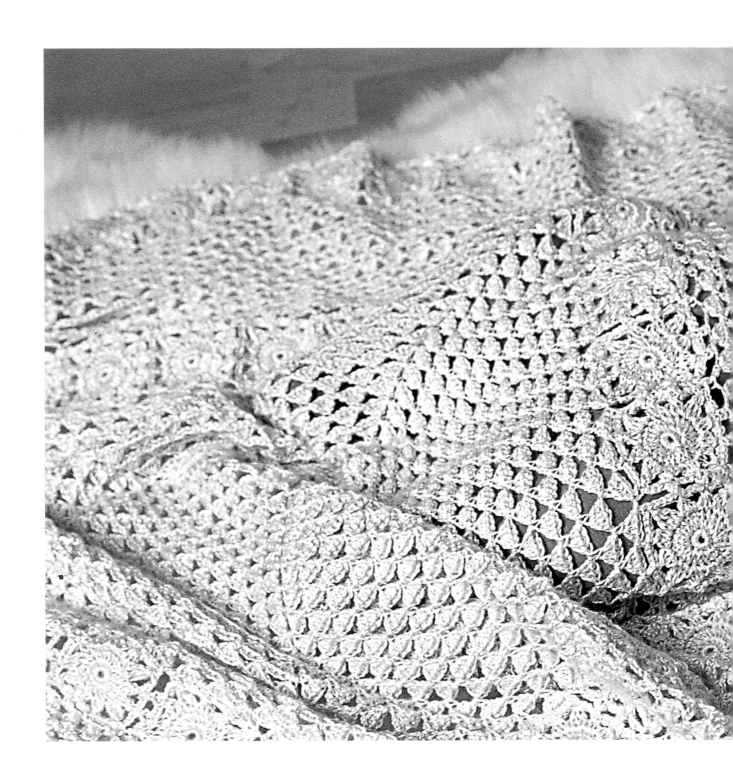

CROCHET
for babies and toddlers

Betty Barnden

Martingale™
& COMPANY

20205 144th Ave. NE
Woodinville, WA 98072-8478 USA
www.martingale-pub.com

Copyright © 2001 text and crochet patterns Betty Barnden
Copyright © 2001 illustrations and photographs
New Holland Publishers (UK) Ltd.
Copyright © 2001 New Holland Publishers (UK) Ltd. All rights reserved.
First published in USA by Martingale & Company. Published in the
United Kingdom by New Holland Publishers (UK) Ltd.

ISBN 1-56477-419-8

Library of Congress Cataloging-in-Publication Data
available upon request.

Designer: Frances de Rees
Photographer: John Freeman
Pattern Checker: Sue Whiting
Diagrams: Steve Dew
Illustrations: Moira McTague
Technical Illustrations: Carrie Hill
Editorial Direction: Rosemary Wilkinson
Editor: Clare Hubbard
Assistant Editor: Emily Preece-Morrison

Reproduction by Pica Digital PTE Ltd, Singapore
Printed and bound in Malaysia by Times Offset (M) Sdn. Bhd.

1 3 5 7 9 10 8 6 4 2

CONTENTS

INTRODUCTION

With a ball or two of yarn and a simple hook you can create pattern and texture in any shape. A few basic stitches, once learned, can be combined in many ways to form beautiful stitch patterns and motifs. Traditionally, crochet work used very fine hooks and cotton or linen threads to make intricate patterns in imitation of handmade lace for articles such as collars, cuffs, and tablecloths. The related technique of Tunisian or Afghan crochet used heavier woolen yarns to create firm, warm fabrics for blankets and coats. While these traditions continue, crochet today also takes advantage of current ranges of knitting yarns, combining color and texture to create easy-to-wear, practical fabrics suitable for all types of garments as well as blankets, toys, and other articles.

Designs in this book include simple, quickly made garments suitable for beginners, such as Two Easy Pullovers and Striped Pullover with Toy Rabbit, and more complicated and challenging designs such as Christening Shawl and Two-Color Pullover. The detailed instructions for each design are accompanied by measurement diagrams and a stitch diagram illustrating with symbols the main stitch/stitches used. Actual measurements for each garment are located in the project size charts, so you can choose which size will best suit your needs. If in doubt, make a larger size.

The basic crochet stitches used in the designs are described in detail along with tips for finishing. Various special techniques are covered, including intarsia (used for the Polar Bear Jacket and the Sleeping Bag), woven crochet (Tartan Cropped Jacket and Beret), and filet crochet (Rabbit Curtain). Appliqué motifs such as flowers, stars, and snowflakes can be used to decorate any garment. For example, you could personalize your design by stitching little flower motifs from the Jumper onto the Lacy Cardigan, or a rabbit motif from the Nursery Pillow onto the Overalls.

Whether you are making a practical outfit for a new baby or a gift for a special occasion such as a christening or birthday, there's a whole range of designs and items from which to choose. I hope you will enjoy making these designs as much as your family and friends will enjoy receiving and using them.

SUBSTITUTING YARNS

If you cannot obtain the yarn specified for a pattern, try to find an alternative of the same weight and fiber content. Fingering-weight yarns are likely to be equivalent to three-ply or four-ply. *Sport* or *worsted* may often be substituted for DK (double knitting). Be sure to check your gauge with the new yarn very carefully if you are making a garment; for toys and other accessories the finished size is not so crucial. For larger projects, it is a good idea to buy just one ball of substitute yarn and try to obtain the correct gauge before buying all the yarn. The amount of substitute yarn required may vary from the amount quoted in the pattern.

BASICS

YARNS

Most of the designs in this book are worked in knitting yarns particularly suited to babies' and children's garments, being machine-washable, soft, and non-irritating to sensitive skins. Other yarns used consist of natural fibers such as cotton and silk, with a smooth, soft finish. If possible, always use the brand of yarn specified in the instructions. Resource information appears on page 112.

HOOKS

Size ranges from Europe, the UK, and the US do not directly correspond, so instructions can be confusing and substitution very difficult. Therefore, this book quotes only hook sizes in millimeters.

Smaller sizes of hooks are normally made of aluminum and larger sizes of plastic, wood, or bamboo. The hooks must be smooth with no nicks or scratches, so it is worth replacing old hooks from time to time.

Crochet hooks are manufactured in a range of sizes and are usually made from aluminum, plastic, wood, or bamboo.

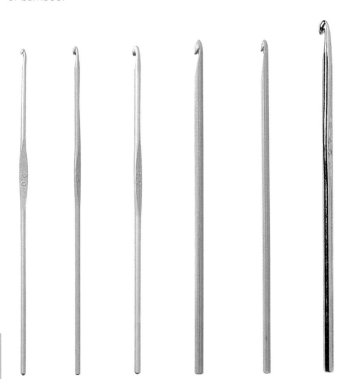

FIRST STEPS

HOLD THE HOOK AND YARN

For practicing crochet, use a substantial yarn such as double knitting, with an appropriate hook such as size 4.00 mm. If you are left handed, try propping the book next to a mirror so you can read the text but also look at the illustrations in reverse.

You may hold the hook in one of two ways; choose whichever you find the most natural: hold it as you would a pencil (fig. 1) or as you would a knife (fig. 2). Place the ball of yarn to your left.

Fig. 1

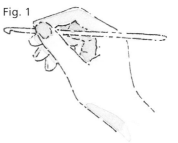

Fig. 2

MAKE A CHAIN (abbreviation: ch)

1. First make a slip knot about 4" from the beginning of the yarn by making a loop and using the hook to draw another loop through it (fig. 3). Gently tighten the knot and slide it up to the hook (fig. 4).

Fig. 3

Fig. 4

2. The left hand holds the work and controls the yarn. There are several ways to hold the yarn with the fingers, but this method gives good control. Wrap the yarn around the little finger to keep it from slipping. Then wrap the yarn over the index finger, which can control the position of the yarn relative to the hook (fig. 5).

Fig. 5

3. Hold the slip knot between the thumb and middle finger of the left hand, use the hook to catch the yarn next to the index finger, and pull a loop through the slip knot to make a new loop on the hook (fig. 6). 1 chain made. Do not pull too tightly.

Fig. 6

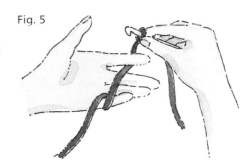

4. Always holding the work close to the hook, repeat step 3 to length required (fig. 7). All the chains should be the same size and not too tight.

5. To fasten off, cut the yarn about 4" from the hook and pull the yarn end through the last loop on the hook.

Fig. 7

9

BASIC STITCHES

Stitches worked in rows usually begin with a base chain of a specific number of stitches. Do not count the slip knot as the first chain or the loop on the hook as a chain. It is best to count the chains as you make them, and then lay the work flat (without twisting) and count them again.

When working into a base chain, you may insert the hook either under the single top thread of each chain or under the top two threads of each chain (which is sometimes easier to see). Decide which method is easier for you and be consistent.

When you reach the end of a row, turn the work clockwise to prevent twisting the edge stitches.

Try out the following basic stitches, beginning with a base chain of about 20 chains:

SINGLE CROCHET (abbreviation: sc)

Row 1: insert hook in second ch from hook, wrap yarn around hook (yo) (fig. 8), and pull a loop of yarn through this ch (2 loops on hook). Yo again (fig. 9) and pull another loop through both loops on hook. 1 sc made (fig. 10). Work 1 sc in each ch to end (do not work into the slip knot) and turn the work.
Row 2: ch 1, insert hook under 2 threads at top of first sc (fig. 11) and work 1 sc, then work 1 sc in each sc to end of row. Turn. Repeat row 2. There should be the same number of sc on each row.

Fig. 8

Fig. 9

Fig. 10

Fig. 11

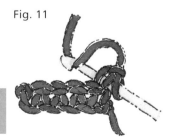

The ch 1 at the beginning of each row is called a turning chain. Different stitches require different numbers of turning chains, as given below.

When working rows of single crochet, always begin each row in the first single crochet and do not work into the turning chain at the end. Do not count the turning chain as a stitch.

HALF DOUBLE CROCHET (abbreviation: hdc)

Row 1: yo in the direction shown and insert hook in third ch from hook (fig. 12), pull a

Fig. 12

loop of yarn through this ch only (3 loops on hook), and yo (fig. 13). Pull this loop through all 3 loops on hook (fig. 14). 1 hdc made. Work 1 hdc in each ch to end, turn the work.
Row 2: ch 2, insert hook under 2 threads at top of first hdc, and work 1 hdc. Then work 1 hdc in each hdc to end of row, turn. Repeat row 2.

Fig. 13

Fig. 14

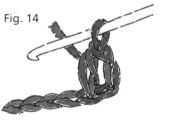

DOUBLE CROCHET (abbreviation: dc)

Row 1: yo in the direction shown and insert hook in 4th ch from hook (fig. 15), pull a loop of yarn through this ch only (3 loops on hook), and yo again (fig. 16). Pull this loop

Fig. 15

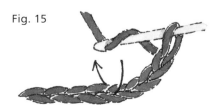

Fig. 16

Fig. 17

Fig. 18

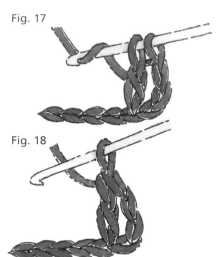

through the first 2 loops on hook and yo again (fig. 17). Pull this loop through the remaining 2 loops on hook (fig. 18). 1 dc made. Work 1 dc in each ch to end, turn the work.
Row 2: ch 3, skip first dc of previous row, insert hook under 2 threads at top of next dc, and work 1 dc in each dc, ending with 1 dc in third ch of ch 3 at beginning of previous row, turn.
Repeat row 2.

Depending on the yarn, hook, and firmness of fabric required, rows of double crochets are sometimes worked with two turning chains instead of three for a neater edge. Always follow the instructions in any particular pattern or shaping may be affected. The two or three turning chains are usually counted as the first stitch of the row.

Always work the first double crochet of a row into the second double crochet of the previous row, and always work the last double crochet of a row into the top of the turning chain at the beginning of the previous row.

OTHER COMMON STITCHES

TREBLE (abbreviation: tr)

Yo twice, insert hook as directed, yo, pull this loop through work only (4 loops on hook), yo, pull this loop through first 2 loops on hook, yo, pull this loop through next 2 loops on hook, yo, pull this loop through remaining 2 loops on hook. 1 tr made.

SLIP STITCH (abbreviation: sl st)
Insert hook as directed, yo, pull this loop through work and through loop on hook in one movement. 1 sl st made.

This is a very short stitch used to close a ring of chains or a round of crochet. It is also used sometimes to work along the edge of a piece and take the yarn to another position without adding any bulk to the fabric.

Most stitch patterns in this book are combinations of the previously mentioned stitches. Other stitches used are described as they occur.

FASTENING OFF

At the end of a piece, work 1 chain, cut yarn at least 4" from the work and pull through the last chain. Longer ends may be left if required for finishing.

To fasten off when working in rounds, work the last slip stitch as instructed and cut the yarn, leaving an end of at least 4", and pull the cut end through the work. Insert the hook in the same place, from the back of the work through to the front, catch the cut end, and pull it through to the wrong side.

GAUGE

It is most important to check your gauge before beginning to work from any pattern. Gauge varies not only with the yarn and hook size used, but also with the hands of the individual crocheter. The number of stitches and rows given in any crochet pattern have been carefully calculated according to the gauge quoted in that pattern, so if your gauge is too loose your work will be too big, and if your gauge is too tight your work will be too small. A difference of just one stitch in 4" can result in a variation of several inches over a whole garment.

Each design in this book recommends a gauge for the main stitch used. Using the yarn and hook size given, work a sample piece at least 6" square. Press the sample as instructed on the yarn label. When working with acrylic yarn, it is advisable to leave the sample for a few hours or overnight before measuring the gauge; measurements may vary as the yarn relaxes.

Lay the sample on a flat surface and insert two pins 4" apart along a straight row of stitches and away from the edges of the sample, measuring with a ruler or tape measure (fig. 19). Count the number of stitches between the pins. Then insert two pins 4" apart, one above the other, and count the number of rows between them (fig. 20).

If your work has more stitches or rows than the given gauge, your gauge is too tight and you should make another sample piece with a larger hook size.

TIPS

● Some balls of yarn may be unwound by pulling the thread out from the center, which prevents the ball from rolling around as you work. Yarn wound onto a cardboard (or other) center may be pulled out from a small plastic bag, loosely closed with a rubber band, to prevent soiling.

● Always join a new ball of yarn at the beginning of a row, never in the middle. To avoid having to unravel the work, try this technique: when you think you have enough yarn left for two rows, tie a loose slip knot at the center of the remaining yarn and work one row. If you have to unpick the knot, there isn't enough yarn left for another row.

● Count stitches, rows, and rounds carefully. Plastic coil rings are available in various sizes and colors to use as markers (fig. 21) or you can use short lengths of contrasting yarn tied into loops. When working several repeats of rows, for example on a sleeve shaping, it is a good idea to make a note of each row as you complete it.

Fig. 21

● When working two matching pieces such as sleeves to a given length, make a note of the number of rows worked on the first piece; then make the second piece exactly the same.

● When measuring the length as work progresses, lay it on a flat surface and measure at the center, not at a side edge.

● When working with dark colors, it can be difficult to see the stitches, especially by artificial light. Try placing a bulb in your lamp that imitates natural light and cover your lap with a white cloth.

Fig. 19

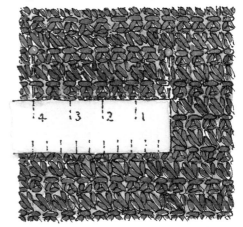

Fig. 20

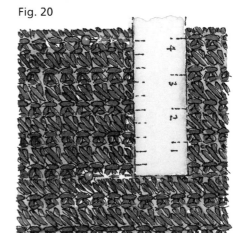

If your work has fewer stitches or rows than the given gauge, your gauge is too loose and you should try again with a smaller hook size.

11

FINISHING

Always use a blunt-ended needle (sold as a tapestry or yarn needle) to avoid splitting the yarn. These needles are available in various sizes to suit different thicknesses of yarn. As a rule, sew with the yarn used for the garment, which will help avoid problems when the garment is washed. If the yarn is thick, try splitting it into two thinner threads, or use a finer matching yarn of the same fiber content.

Seams on baby garments should not be lumpy or bulky. Try the following method, which is neat and presses flat, to avoid these kinds of problems.

WOVEN FLAT SEAM

Hold the two pieces to be joined with right sides together and the left forefinger between them as shown. Insert the needle from the front through both pieces just below corresponding stitches and pull it through to the back. Insert the needle from the back through both pieces just below the next pair of corresponding stitches and pull it through to the front (fig. 22). Make each stitch quite small. To join rows of single crochet work about one stitch per row; for rows of double crochet, work two or three stitches per row. Match the ends of the rows carefully. Pull the yarn tightly for a neat finish. Press the seam open following the instructions on the yarn label.

Fig. 22

YARN ENDS

Yarn ends should never be secured with a knot. Use a blunt-ended needle to run them in either along the back of a row of stitches or along the wrong side of a seam line, for at least 2"; then trim off the excess yarn. When working a border, it is often possible to work over any yarn ends and enclose them within the border stitches for at least 2". After completing the border, pull gently on the yarn ends to tighten them, and trim off the excess.

BUTTONS AND FASTENINGS

It is best to purchase buttons after completing a garment to make sure they fit the buttonholes snugly. Many of the fancy shaped buttons available are not really suitable for crocheted (or knitted) garments because they are liable to catch on the yarn. Choose smooth, round buttons.

Lay the garment on a flat surface and place the buttonhole band over the button band, matching the edges and pattern exactly. Insert pins at right angles to the button band, through the center of each buttonhole. Sew a button at each marked position in the center of the button band, using the same yarn as the garment or matching sewing thread.

Another closure option is plastic snap fasteners, which are more suitable than metal ones for baby garments. Sew them on with matching sewing thread, taking four or five tiny stitches through each hole around the edge of each half of the fastener.

PRESSING

Washing and pressing instructions are normally printed on yarn labels. Don't throw all the yarn labels away! File one for future reference. As a general guide, natural fibers (wool, cotton, silk) may be pressed under a damp cloth with a warm iron. Do not overpress textured patterns. Synthetic fibers may be pressed under a dry cloth with a moderate or cool iron. Some require no pressing at all. If in doubt, use your gauge sample as a test piece.

It is a good idea to make a collection of all your gauge samples and attach a label of the yarn used.

EMBROIDERY

Simple embroidery is used to decorate some of the designs in this book. Use a blunt-ended needle to avoid splitting stitches and work quite loosely so the project remains flat.

Fig. 23

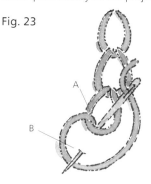

Chain Stitch (fig. 23)

Bring thread out at A and hold down with left thumb. Insert needle back in same hole and bring the point out a short distance

away at B. Pull thread through, keeping loop under needle point. Repeat to length of chain required and end with a small stitch to secure the last loop.

Fig. 24

Single Chain Stitch (Fig. 24)

This stitch, sometimes called the lazy daisy stitch, is worked in the same way as the chain stitch, but each loop is secured with a small stitch.

Fig. 25

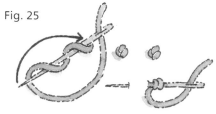

French Knot (Fig. 25)

Bring needle out at front. Wind yarn around the needle twice; then hold thread down with left thumb and insert needle close to where it emerged. Pull thread through to the back. Repeat as required.

Fig. 26

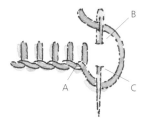

Blanket Stitch (fig. 26)

Work from left to right. Bring needle out at A. *Hold thread down with left thumb and insert needle at B, bringing it out at C, over the loop of thread. Pull needle through and repeat from * as required.

Strawberry motif on Strawberry Pullover

WORKING IN ROUNDS

Sometimes crochet is not worked back and forth in rows, but in rounds. Flat geometric shapes (circles, squares, and hexagons) begin at the center with a small ring of chain stitches (fig. 27). Each round is normally worked counter-clockwise, with the right side of work facing, and begins with a number of chains as a substitute for the first stitch and ends with a slip stitch into one of these chains to close the round.

Fig. 27

Bowl shapes such as hats are also worked in rounds to avoid seams. Depending on the stitch used, the rounds may be worked in a continuous spiral to keep the pattern uniform all over. For accuracy, place a stitch marker on the first stitch of each round, moving it up from round to round as work proceeds. Cuffs and borders are often worked in rounds to make neat edges.

WORKING FROM CHARTS

INTARSIA

This is a method of working a design from a chart in two or more colors, using a separate ball of yarn for each area of color. Colors are never passed across the back of the work from one area to another.

The chart shows the right side of the work and each small square (or rectangle) represents one stitch. Begin at the bottom of the chart and read right side rows (odd numbers) from right to left and wrong side rows (even numbers) from left to right.

Count the stitches carefully and change colors where required as follows:

To Change Colors in Double Crochet

Begin the last stitch in the old color: yo, insert hook, pull through, yo, pull through first 2 loops on hook, change to new color, yo, pull new color through 2 loops on hook (fig. 28). Leave old color at wrong side.

Fig. 28

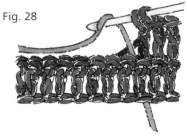

To Change Colors in Half Double Crochet

Begin the last stitch in the old color: yo, insert hook, pull old color through, change to new color, yo, pull new color through 3 loops on hook. Leave old color at wrong side of work

On subsequent rows the old color may not be in the right position for the color change. If the new color change comes before the old color change, the new color may be loosely stranded across a few stitches and this "float" caught later when weaving in the ends. If the interval is more than a few stitches, cut the yarn and rejoin it in the new position; otherwise the work may be pulled out of shape.

If the new color change comes after the old color change, stitches may be worked over the new color to enclose it and bring it to the new position. This should only be done along the outline of the design; otherwise the new color may show through.

FILET CROCHET

This technique uses a regular mesh pattern with certain squares filled to form the design. Each square on a filet crochet chart represents either a mesh square or a block, not a single stitch (see page 100 for a chart example). A typical mesh square might be formed by working ch 1, skip 1 st, 1 dc in next st; a block might be formed by working 1 dc in each of next 2 sts.

Begin at the bottom of the chart and read right-side rows (odd numbers) from right to left and wrong-side rows (even numbers) from left to right. For each row, work the turning chain given; then work each square on the chart as either a mesh square or a block.

COMMON ABBREVIATIONS

alt alternate; **approx** approximate; **beg** beginning; **ch** chain; **col** color; **cont** continue; **dc** double crochet; **dc2tog** double crochet 2 together=[yo, insert hook in next st, yo, pull through a loop, yo, pull through 2 lps] twice, yo, pull through all lps on hook; **dc3tog** double crochet 3 together=as dc2tog but rep [ ] 3 times in all; **dc4tog** double crochet 4 together=as dc2tog but rep [ ] 4 times in all; **dc5tog** double crochet 5 together=as dc2tog but rep [ ] 5 times in all; **dec** decrease; **foll** following; **hdc** half double crochet; **hdc2tog** half double crochet 2 together=[yo, insert hook in next st, pull through a lp] twice, yo, pull through all lps on hook; **hdc3tog** half double crochet 3 together=as hdc2tog but rep [ ] 3 times in all; **inc** increase; **lp** loop; **patt** pattern; **rem** remaining; **rep** repeat; **RS** right side; **sc** single crochet; **sc2tog** single crochet 2 together= [insert hook in next st, yo, pull through a lp] twice, yo, pull through all lps on hook; **sc3tog** single crochet 3 together= as sc2tog but rep [ ] 3 times in all; **sp** space; **sl st** slip stitch; **st(s)** stitch(es); **tog** together; **tr** treble; **tr2tog** treble 2 together=[yo twice, insert hook in next st, yo, pull through a lp, yo, pull through 2 lps, yo, pull through 2 lps] twice, yo, pull through all lps on hook; **tr3tog** treble 3 together=as tr2tog but rep [ ] 3 times in all; **tr7tog** treble 7 together=as tr2tog but rep [ ] 7 times in all; **WS** wrong side; **yo** yarn around hook.

STITCH DIAGRAMS

Each pattern in this book is accompanied by one or more stitch diagrams, visual forms of the main stitch patterns used and intended as an addition to the written instructions, which should always be read carefully.

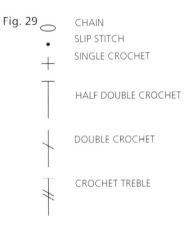

Fig. 29
CHAIN
SLIP STITCH
SINGLE CROCHET
HALF DOUBLE CROCHET
DOUBLE CROCHET
CROCHET TREBLE

Stitches worked in the same place are shown joined at the base.

e.g. = 2 half double crochets into 1 chain

Two or more stitches worked together are shown joined at the top

e.g. = 3 double crochets together

Key to Stitch Diagrams (fig.29).

Note that symbols may be squashed or stretched to fit the diagrams.

PATTERN NOTES

1. Figures in parentheses ( ) refer to the larger sizes. If only one set of figures is given, it refers to all sizes.
2. Instructions in brackets [ ] should be done together as given or repeated the number of times given after the brackets.

WRAPAROUND TOP, SHORTS, AND HAT

THIS PRACTICAL YET BEAUTIFUL OUTFIT IS GREAT FOR ANY
NEW BABY: EASY TO PUT ON, SOFT AND WARM TO WEAR.

SIZES (see also page 16)

APPROXIMATE AGES	1 mo	1–2 mos	2–3 mos
TOP			
to fit chest	12"	14"	16"
actual measurement	14"	16"	18¼"
length to shoulder	7½"	8½"	9½"
sleeve seam	3¾"	4½"	5¼"
SHORTS			
to fit hips	12"	14"	16"
HAT			
to fit head	15"	16"	17"

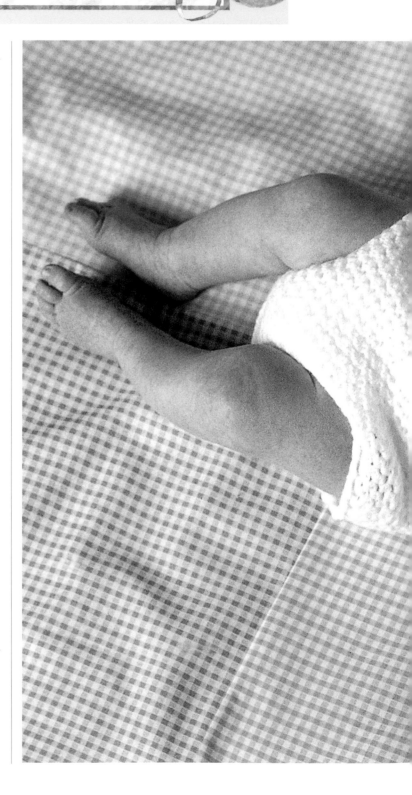

MATERIALS FOR THE SET

3 (3, 3) balls of Fairytale 3-ply by Patons for the set (100%
acrylic, 50g/178yds), col 3300 Snow White *or* comparable yarn
2.00 mm and 2.50 mm hooks
2 snap fasteners or 3 ft narrow ribbon for top
Shirring elastic and 3 snap fasteners for shorts

GAUGE

Top and Shorts: 12 patts and 19 rows = 4" in between
stitch with size 2.50 mm hook
Hat: First 4 rounds = 1½" in diameter with size 2.50 mm
hook

WRAPAROUND TOP INSTRUCTIONS

NOTE
For minimal seams, the body is worked in 1 piece up to the
armholes and the yoke is worked in 1 piece across the body and
sleeves.

SLEEVES (make 2)
With size 2.50 mm hook, ch 29 (33, 37).

Row 1 (RS row): 2 hdc in third ch from hook, *skip 1 ch, 2 hdc in next ch, rep from * to end, turn—14 (16, 18) patts.

Row 2 (between stitch): ch 2, *skip 2 hdc, 2 hdc in sp before next 2 hdc, rep from *, ending 2 hdc under ch 2 at beg previous row, turn.

Rep this row twice more. 4 rows in all.

Sleeve Shaping

Row 5: ch 3, 2 hdc in third ch from hook, work patt as set to end, turn.

Row 6: work as for row 5—16 (18, 20) patts.

Rows 7 and 8 (7–10, 7–12): rep row 2 a total of 2 (4, 6) times. Rep rows 5–8 (5–10, 5–12) once more, and then rows 5 and 6 once again—20 (22, 24) patts; 14 (18, 22) rows in all.

BETWEEN STITCH

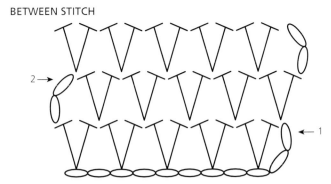

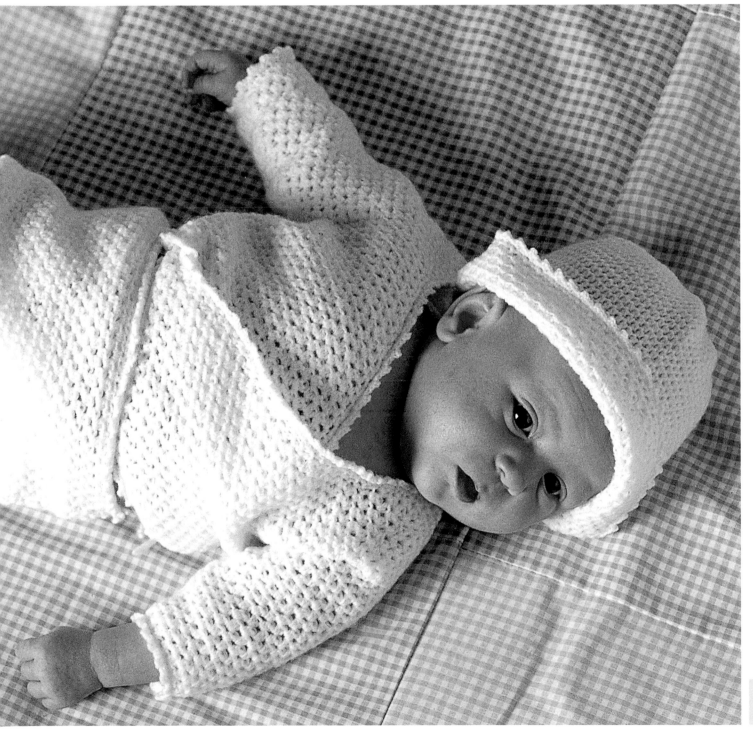

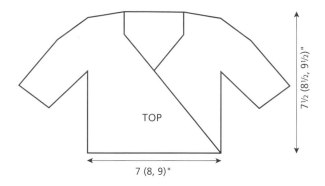

TOP

7½ (8½, 9½)"

7 (8, 9)"

9 (10¼, 11)"

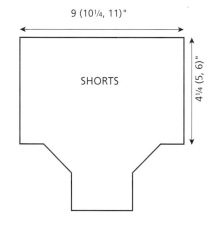

SHORTS

4¼ (5, 6)"

Rep row 2 a total of 3 more times. 17 (21, 25) rows in all, ending with a RS row. Fasten off.

BODY
With size 2.50 mm hook, ch 129 (149, 169).
Work as for row 1 of sleeves—64 (74, 84) patts.

Front Edge Shaping
Row 2: ch 2, skip 2 hdc, 1 hdc in next sp (counts as first patt), *skip 2 hdc, 2 hdc in next sp, rep from *, ending 1 hdc in last sp, 1 hdc under ch 2 at beg previous row (last 2 hdc count as last patt), turn—63 (73, 83) patts.
Rep this row 19 (21, 23) more times—44 (52, 60) patts; 21 (23, 25) rows in all, ending with a RS row. Do not fasten off but cont:

YOKE
Row 1: ch 2, skip 2 hdc, 1 hdc in next sp, work 8 (10, 12) patts as set, then with WS of first sleeve facing work across top edge: skip first 4 hdc, 2 hdc in next sp, work 16 (18, 20) patts as set leaving 4 hdc at end. Cont along top edge of body: skip next 8 hdc, 2 hdc in next sp, work 18 (22, 26) patts as set, then work across top edge of second sleeve in same way as first. Cont along top edge of body: skip next 8 hdc, 2 hdc in next sp, work 7 (9, 11) patts as set, 1 hdc in last sp, 1 hdc under ch 2 at beg previous row, turn—71 (83, 95) patts.
Row 2: ch 2, skip 2 hdc, 1 hdc in next sp, *work patt as set to sp between body and sleeve, 1 hdc in this sp, rep from * 3 more times, work patt as set, ending 1 hdc in last sp, 1 hdc under ch 2, turn.
Row 3: ch 2, skip 2 hdc, 1 hdc in next sp, *work patt as set to sp before single hdc, hdc2tog over this sp and next sp, rep from * 3 more times, work patt as set, ending 1 hdc in last sp, 1 hdc under ch 2, turn.
Row 4: ch 2, skip 2 hdc, 1 hdc in next sp, *work patt as set to sp

before hdc2tog, hdc2tog over this sp and next sp, rep from * 3 more times, work patt as set, ending 1 hdc in last sp, 1 hdc under ch 2, turn.
Rep row 4 a total of 2 (4, 6) more times.
Next row: dec at armhole positions only: ch 2, skip 2 hdc, *work patt as set to sp before hdc2tog, hdc2tog over this sp and next sp, rep from * 3 more times, work patt as set, ending 2 hdc in last sp, 2 hdc under ch 2, turn.
Rep this row 5 more times.
Next row: ch 2, *hdc2tog over next 2 sps, work patt as set to sp before hdc2tog, rep from * twice, hdc2tog over next 2 sps, 2 hdc under ch 2, turn.
Foll row: ch 2, *hdc2tog over next 2 sps, work patt as set to sp before next hdc2tog, rep from * twice, hdc2tog over last sp and under ch 2. Fasten off.
Join sleeve and underarm seams.

CUFFS (make 2)
With RS of sleeve facing and size 2.00 mm hook, join yarn at base of sleeve seam.
Round 1: ch 1, 1 sc in base of each ch all around, ending 1 sl st in ch 1 at beg of round.
Round 2: *ch 2, 1 sl st in st at base of ch 2 (a picot made), 1 sc in each of next 2 sc, rep from * all round, ending 1 sl st in base of ch 2 at beg of round. Fasten off.

FRONT, NECK, AND LOWER EDGE BORDER
With RS facing, and size 2.00 mm hook, join yarn at lower edge below 1 sleeve.
Round 1: ch 1, 1 sc in base of each ch to corner, 4 sc in same place at corner, 3 sc in side edge of every 2 rows up front edge, 1 sc in each hdc along neck edge, working sc2tog at each corner of back neck; 3 sc in side edge of every 2 rows down front edge to corner, 4 sc in same place at corner, 1 sc in base of each ch, ending 1 sl st in ch 1 at beg of round.
Round 2: work as for round 2 of cuff, with 1 extra picot at each front corner.

FINISHING
Fronts may be overlapped in either direction as required. Sew on snaps at corners to fasten, or stitch ribbon ties, length approximately 10", as desired. Press as instructed on yarn labels.

SHORTS INSTRUCTIONS

BACK
With size 2.50 mm hook, ch 21 (23, 25).
Row 1: 2 hdc in third ch from hook, *skip 1 ch, 2 hdc in next ch, rep from * to end, turn—10 (11, 12) patts.
Row 2 (between stitch): ch 2, *skip 2 hdc, 2 hdc in sp before next 2 hdc, rep from *, ending 2 hdc under ch 2 at beg previous row, turn. **
Rep this row 6 (8, 10) more times—8 (10, 12) rows in all.
***Leg Shaping
Inc row: ch 3, 2 hdc in third ch from hook, work patt as set, ending 2 hdc under ch 2, turn—11 (12, 13) patts.
Rep this row 9 more times—20 (21, 22) patts.
Next row: ch 9 (11, 13), 2 hdc in third ch from hook, [skip 1 ch, 2 hdc in next ch] 3 (4, 5) times, work patt as set, ending 2 hdc under ch 2, turn—24 (26, 28) patts.
Rep this row once more—28 (31, 34) patts.
Rep row 2 until straight part of work measures 4 1/4 (5, 6)" from last row of leg shaping, ending WS row.
Fasten off.

HAT INSTRUCTIONS

Round 1: with size 2.50 mm hook, ch 5 and join into a ring with 1 sl st in first ch made.

Round 2: ch 2, 11 hdc into ring, 1 sl st under ch 2—12 sts.

Round 3: ch 2, [2 hdc in next hdc] 11 times, hdc in st at base of ch 2, 1 sl st in second ch of ch 2—24 sts.

Round 4: ch 2, [1 hdc in next hdc, 2 hdc in foll hdc] 11 times, 1 hdc in next hdc, 1 hdc in st at base of ch 2, 1 sl st in second ch of ch 2—36 sts. Check gauge here: pull gently on starting end of yarn to tighten center. First 4 rounds should measure 1½" in diameter.

Round 5. ch 2, *[1 hdc in next hdc] twice, 2 hdc in foll hdc, rep from * 10 more times, [1 hdc in next hdc] twice, 1 hdc in st at base of ch 2, 1 sl st in second ch of ch 2—48 sts.

Round 6: ch 2, *[1 hdc in next hdc] 3 times, 2 hdc in foll hdc, rep from * 10 more times, [1 hdc in next hdc] 3 times, 1 hdc in st at base of ch 2, 1 sl st in second ch of ch 2—60 sts.

Round 7: ch 2, *[1 hdc in next hdc] 4 times, 2 hdc in foll hdc, rep from * 10 more times, [1 hdc in next hdc] 4 times, 1 hdc in st at base of ch 2, 1 sl st in second ch of ch 2—72 sts.

Round 8: ch 2, *[1 hdc in next hdc] 5 times, 2 hdc in foll hdc, rep from * 10 more times, [1 hdc in next hdc] 5 times, 1 hdc in st at base of ch 2, 1 sl st in second ch of ch 2—84 sts.

Second Size Only

Round 9: ch 2, *[1 hdc in next hdc] 13 times, 2 hdc in foll hdc, rep from * 4 more times, [1 hdc in next hdc] 13 times, 1 hdc in st at base of ch 2, 1 sl st in second ch of ch 2—90 sts.

Third Size Only

Round 9: ch 2, *[1 hdc in next hdc] 6 times, 2 hdc in foll hdc, rep from * 10 more times, [1 hdc in next hdc] 6 times, 1 hdc in st at base of ch 2, 1 sl st in second ch of ch 2—96 sts.

All Sizes

84 (90, 96) sts.

Next round: ch 2, 1 hdc in each hdc, ending 1 sl st in second ch of ch 2. Rep this round until work measures 4 (4¾, 5½)" from center to outside edge, ending with a complete round.

BRIM

Brim round 1: ch 2, [1 hdc in each of next 13 (14, 15) hdc, 2 hdc in next hdc] 5 times, 1 hdc in each of next 13 (14, 15) hdc, 1 hdc in st at base of ch 2, 1 sl st in second ch of ch 2—90 (96, 102) sts.

Brim round 2: ch 2, skip 2 hdc, *2 hdc in sp before next hdc, skip 2 hdc, rep from *, ending 1 hdc in base of ch 2, 1 sl st in second ch of ch 2.

Brim round 3: ch 2, 1 hdc in sp at base of ch 2, *skip 2 hdc, 2 hdc in sp before next hdc, rep from *, ending 1 sl st in second ch of ch 2. Rep brim rounds 2 and 3 until brim measures 1½ (1¾, 2)", ending with a complete round.

Next round: ch 1, 1 sc in each hdc, ending 1 sl st in ch 1.

Foll round: *ch 2, 1 sl st in st at base of ch 2 (a picot made), 1 sc in each of next 2 sc, rep from * all around, ending 1 sl st in base of ch 2 at beg of round. Fasten off. Press as instructed on yarn label.

FRONT

Work as for back to **.

Rep row 2 a total of 2 (4, 6) more times—4 (6, 8) rows in all.

Work as for back from *** to end.

WAISTBAND

Join side seams. With shirring elastic doubled, make a ring to fit comfortably around waist, knotting securely and leaving ends at least 2" long.

With RS facing, and size 2.50 mm hook, join yarn to top of 1 side seam.

Round 1: ch 1, *1 sc over elastic ring and into next hdc, rep from *, ending 1 sl st in ch 1 at beg of round. (Work over ends of knot at same time.)

Round 2: *ch 2, 1 sl st in st at base of the ch 2 (a picot made), 1 sc in each of next 2 sc, rep from * all around, ending 1 sl st in base of ch 2 at beg of round. Fasten off.

LEG AND CROTCH BORDER

With RS facing and 2.00 mm hook, join yarn at base of 1 side seam.

Round 1: ch 1, *[1 sc in base of next ch, sc2tog over base of next 2 ch] 2 (3, 3) times, 1 sc in base of each of next 1 (0, 2) ch, 1 sc in side edge of each row to corner, 3 sc in same place at corner, 1 sc in base of each ch across crotch, 3 sc in same place at corner, 1 sc in side edge of each row, 1 sc in base of each of next 1 (0, 2) ch, [sc2tog over base of next 2 ch, 1 sc in next ch] 2 (3, 3) times to side seam, rep from * once more, ending 1 sl st in ch 1 at beg of round.

Round 2: *[ch 2, 1 sl st in st at base of ch 2, 1 sc in each of next 2 sc] to first corner, 3 sc in same place at corner, 1 sc in each sc across straight edge of crotch, 3 sc in same place at corner, rep from * once more, rep [ ], ending 1 sl st in base of ch 2 at beg of round. Fasten off.

FINISHING

Place back crotch over front and sew on 3 snaps to fasten. Press as instructed on yarn labels.

JACKET, PANTS, AND BOOTIES

WARM AS TOAST! THIS SNUG AND PRACTICAL OUTFIT FEATURES
EASY SNAP FASTENERS ON THE PANTS.

SIZES (see also page 20)

APPROXIMATE AGES	1–2 mos	2–3 mos	3–6 mos
JACKET to fit chest	14"	16"	18"
actual measurement	15¾"	18"	20½"
length to back neck	7½"	9"	11"
sleeve seam with cuff folded back	4¾"	5½"	6¾"

APPROXIMATE AGES	1–2 mos	2–3 mos	3–6 mos
PANTS to fit hips	16"	18"	20"
actual measurement	20"	21¾"	23¼"
length to front waist	12"	13"	14¼"
BOOTIES to fit foot length	3"	3½"	4"

MATERIALS

JACKET
2 (2, 2) balls of Snuggly 4-ply by Sirdar (55% nylon, 45% acrylic, 50g/249yds), col 252 Lemon *or* comparable yarn
5 (5, 6) buttons
3.50 mm and 3.00 mm hooks
PANTS
2 (2, 3) balls of Snuggle 4-ply by Sirdar, col 252 Lemon
Shirring elastic
7 (7, 9) snap fasteners
3.50 mm and 3.00 mm hooks
BOOTIES
1 (1, 1) ball of Snuggly 4-ply by Sirdar, col 252 Lemon
3.50 mm and 3.00 mm hooks
NOTE: for the whole set, only 4 (4, 5) balls will be required.

GAUGE

13 patts and 17 rows = 4" in cluster stitch with size 3.50 mm hook
19 sts and 23 rows = 4" in rows of sc with size 3.50 mm hook

JACKET INSTRUCTIONS

BACK
With size 3.50 mm hook, ch 55 (63, 71).
Foundation row: 1 sc in third ch from hook, *ch 1, skip 1 ch, 1 sc in next ch, rep from * to end, turn.
Patt row (cluster stitch): ch 2, skip first sc, sc2tog over first 2 ch sps, *ch 1, sc2tog over last ch sp used and next ch sp, rep from *, ending sc2tog over last ch-1 sp and ch-2 sp at beg previous row, ch 1, 1 sc in same ch-2 sp, turn—26 (30, 34) patts. (Count each sc2tog as 1 patt.)
Rep this row until back measures 3¼ (4, 4¾)", ending WS row.

CLUSTER STITCH

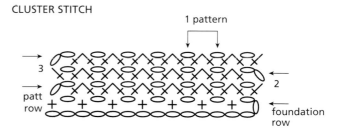

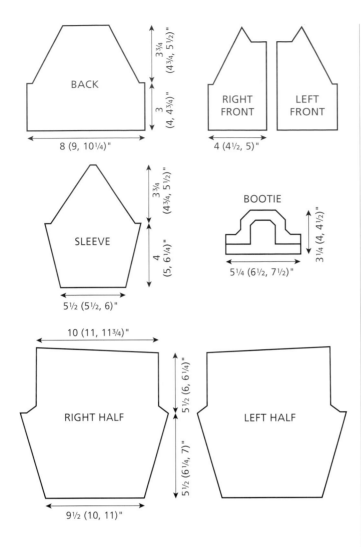

BACK

3¾
(4¾, 5½)"

3
(4, 4¾)"

8 (9, 10¼)"

RIGHT
FRONT

LEFT
FRONT

4 (4½, 5)"

SLEEVE

3¾
(4¾, 5½)"

4
(5, 6¼)"

5½ (5½, 6)"

BOOTIE

3¼ (4, 4½)"

5¼ (6½, 7½)"

10 (11, 11¾)"

RIGHT HALF

LEFT HALF

5½ (6, 6¼)"

5½ (6¼, 7)"

9½ (10, 11)"

Raglan Armhole Shaping

Dec row 1: sl st across [ch 1, sc2tog] twice, ch 2, work patt until 22 (26, 30) patts are complete, ch 1, 1 sc in next sc2tog, turn leaving [ch 1, sc2tog, ch 2] unworked.

Dec row 2: work as for patt row.

Dec row 3: work patt as set, ending sc2tog over last ch-1 sp and ch-2 sp at beg previous row, turn.

Dec row 4: ch 2, skip sc2tog, work patt as set, ending sc2tog over last ch-1 sp and ch-2 sp at beg previous row, turn.

Dec row 5: ch 2, skip sc2tog, work patt as set, ending as end of patt row, turn—20 (24, 28) patts.

Second and Third Sizes Only
Dec row 6: work as for patt row.

Second Size Only
Rep dec rows 3–5 once.

Third Size Only
Rep dec rows 3–6 once and 3–5 again.

All Sizes
20 (22, 24) patts.
Rep dec row 3 once.
Rep dec row 4 a total of 9 times—10 (12, 14) patts.
Rep dec row 5 once. Fasten off.

LEFT FRONT
With size 3.50 mm hook, ch 29 (33, 37).
Work foundation row and patt row as for back—13 (15, 17) patts.

Rep patt row until back measures 3¼ (4, 4¾)", ending WS row. **

Raglan Armhole Shaping

Dec row 1: sl st across [ch 1, sc2tog] twice, ch 2, work 11 (13, 15) patts as set to end, turn.

Dec row 2: work as for patt row.

Dec row 3: work as for patt row.

Dec row 4: work patt as set, ending sc2tog over last ch-1 sp and ch-2 sp at beg previous row, turn.

Dec row 5: ch2, skip sc2tog, work patt as set, ending at end of patt row, turn—10 (12, 14) patts.

Second and Third Sizes Only
Dec row 6: work as for patt row.

Second Size Only
Rep dec rows 3–5 once.

Third Size Only
Rep dec rows 3–6 once and 3–5 again.

All Sizes
10 (11, 12) patts.
Rep dec rows 4 and 5 a total of 2 (2, 1) times.
Rep dec row 4 once more—8 (9, 11) patts.

Front Neck Shaping

Row 1: ch 2, skip sc2tog, sc2tog over first 2 ch sps, [ch 1, sc2tog over last ch sp used and next ch sp] 4 (4, 5) times, turn—5 (5, 6) patts.

Row 2: ch 2, skip sc2tog, work patt as set, ending sc2tog over last 2 ch sps, turn—4 (4, 5) patts.

Rows 3 and 4: work as for row 2—2 (2, 3) patts.

Third Size Only
Row 5: work as for dec row 5.

Row 6: work as for dec row 4.

All Sizes
2 patts.

Next row: ch 2, sc2tog over first and last ch sps, ch 1, 1 sc in last ch sp, turn.

Foll row: ch 2, sc2tog over first and last ch sps—1 patt. Fasten off.

RIGHT FRONT
Work as for left front to **.

Raglan Armhole Shaping

Dec row 1: ch 2, work patt until 11 (13, 15) patts are complete, ch 1, 1 sc in next sc2tog, turn, leaving [ch-1 sp, sc2tog, ch 2] unworked.

Dec row 2: as patt row.

Dec row 3: work patt as set, ending sc2tog over last 2 ch sps, turn.

Dec row 4: ch 2, skip sc2tog, work patt as set to end, turn.

Dec rows 5 and 6: as patt row—10 (12, 14) patts.

Second and Third Sizes Only
Rep dec rows 3–6 (once, twice) more.

All Sizes
10 (11, 12) patts.
Rep dec rows 3 and 4 a total of 2 (2, 1) times—8 (9, 11) patts.

Front Neck Shaping

Row 1: sl st across [ch 1, sc2tog] 3 (4, 5) times, ch 2, sc2tog over next 2 ch sps, [ch 1, sc2tog over last ch sp used and next ch sp] 4 (4, 5) times, turn—5 (5, 6) patts.

Row 2: ch 2, skip sc2tog, work patt as set, ending sc2tog over last 2 ch sps, turn—4 (4, 5) patts.

Row 3: work as for row 2.

Row 4: work as for dec row 4—2 (2, 3) patts.

Third Size Only
Row 5: work as for dec row 3.

Row 6: work as for dec row 4.

All Sizes
2 patts.
Next row: work as for dec row 3.
Foll row: ch 2, skip sc2tog, sc2tog over first and last ch sps, ch 1, 1 sc in last ch sp—1 patt. Fasten off.

SLEEVES (make 2)
With size 3.50 mm hook, ch 43 (43, 47).
Work foundation row and patt row as for back—20 (20, 22) patts.
Inc row 1: ch 2, sc2tog over st at base of this ch and first ch sp, work patt as set to end, turn.
Inc row 2: work as for inc row 1—22 (22, 24) patts.
Inc rows 3 and 4: work as for patt row.
Rep these 4 rows 1 (2, 3) more times—24 (26, 30) patts.
Rep inc rows 1 and 2 once more—26 (28, 32) patts.
Rep patt row until sleeve measures 4¼ (5, 6¼)" in all, ending WS row.
Raglan Sleeve Shaping
Dec row 1: sl st across [ch 1, sc2tog] twice, ch 2, work in patt until 22 (24, 28) patts are complete, ch 1, 1 sc in next sc2tog, turn leaving [ch1, sc2tog, ch 2] unworked.
Dec row 2: work as for patt row.
Dec row 3: work patt as set, ending sc2tog over last ch-1 sp and ch-2 sp at beg previous row, turn.
Dec row 4: ch 2, skip first sc2tog, work patt as set, ending sc2tog over last ch-1 sp and ch-2 sp at beg previous row, turn—21 (23, 27) patts.

Rep dec row 4 a total of 5 (11, 15) more times—16 (12, 12) patts.
Next row: ch 2, skip first ch sp, sc2tog over next 2 ch sps, *ch 1, sc2tog over last ch sp used and next ch sp, rep from *, ending sc2tog over last 2 ch sps, turn—14 (10, 10) patts.
Rep this row 6 (4, 4) more times—2 patts. Fasten off.

FINISHING
Join raglan seams. Join side and sleeve seams.
Cuffs (make 2)
With RS facing, and size 3.00 mm hook, join yarn at base of sleeve seam.
Round 1: ch 1, 1 sc in base of each ch, ending 1 sc in first sc of round.
Round 2: 1 sc in each sc all around.
Rep round 2 a total of 5 times, ending at underarm. Fasten off.
Fold cuff back.

Front, Neck, and Lower Border

With RS facing and size 3.00 mm hook, join yarn at base of 1 side seam.

Round 1: ch 1, 1 sc in each ch sp and base of each sc to corner, 3 sc in same place at corner, 1 sc in side edge of each row up right front edge, 3 sc in same place at corner, 42 (50, 58) sc evenly around neck to top of left front edge, 3 sc in same place at corner, 1 sc in side edge of each row down left front edge, 3 sc in same place at corner and 1 sc in each ch sp and base of each sc, ending 1 sl st in first sc of round.

Round 2: ch 1, 1 sc in first sc, 1 sc in each sc, working 3 sc in second of 3 sc at each outer corner, ending skip last sc, 1 sl st in first sc of round.

To button left front over right: round 3: work as for round 2, ending 3 sc in second of 3 sc at top of left front edge, [ch 2, skip 2 sc, 1 sc in each of 4 (5, 5) sc] 4 (4, 5) times, ch 2, skip next 2 sc, complete as round 2.

(To button right front over left: round 3: work as for round 2, ending 3 sc in second of 3 sc at bottom of right front edge, count down 27 (31, 38) sc from second of 3 sc at next corner and place a marker on this st, 1 sc in each sc, ending with marked st, [ch 2, skip 2 sc, 1 sc in each of 4 (5, 5) sc] 4 (4, 5) times, ch 2, skip next 2 sc, complete as round 2.)

Both versions: round 4: ch 1, 1 sc in first sc, 1 sc in each sc, 3 sc in second of 3 sc at each corner and 2 sc in each ch-2 sp, ending skip last sc, 1 sl st in first sc of round. Fasten off.

Sew on buttons to match buttonholes.

Press as instructed on yarn labels.

PANTS INSTRUCTIONS

RIGHT HALF

With size 3.50 mm hook, ch 47 (49, 53).

Foundation row: 1 sc in second ch from hook, 1 sc in each ch to end, turn—46 (48, 52) sc.

Sc row: ch 1, 1 sc in first sc, 1 sc in each sc to end, turn.

Leg Shaping

Inc row 1: ch 1, 2 sc in first sc, 1 sc in each sc to end, turn.

Inc row 2: work as for inc row 1.

Inc rows 3 and 4: work as for sc row—48 (50, 54) sc.

Rep these 4 rows 6 (7, 8) more times—60 (64, 70) sc.

Rep sc row until work measures 5½ (6¼, 7)", ending WS row.

*Place a marker at beg of last row.

Top of Pants Shaping

Row 1: sl st across 4 sc, ch 1, sc2tog over next 2 sc, 1 sc in each sc to last 2 sc, sc2tog, turn.

Row 2: ch 1, sc2tog over first 2 sts, 1 sc in each sc to last 2 sts, sc2tog, turn.

Rep row 2 a total of 2 (2, 3) more times—48 (52, 56) sts.

Rep sc row until work measures 11 (12¼, 13¼)" in all, ending WS row.

Waist Shaping

Waist row 1: ch 1, 1 sc in first sc, 1 sc in each of next 35 (38, 41) sc, 1 sl st in next sc, turn.

Waist row 2: ch 1, skip 1 sl st, 1 sc in each st to end, turn.

Waist row 3: ch 1, 1 sc in first sc, 1 sc in each of next 23 (25, 27) sc, 1 sl st in next sc, turn.

Waist row 4: work as for waist row 2.

Waist row 5: ch 1, 1 sc in first sc, 1 sc in each of next 11 (12, 13) sc, 1 sl st in next sc, turn.

Waist row 6: work as for waist row 2. Fasten off.

LEFT HALF

Work as for right half to *.

Place a marker at end of last row.

Top of Pants Shaping

Row 1: ch 1, sc2tog over first 2 sc, 1 sc in each sc to last 6 sc, sc2tog, turn, leaving last 4 sts unworked.

Row 2: ch 1, sc2tog over first 2 sts, 1 sc in each sc to last 2 sts, sc2tog, turn.

Rep row 2 a total of 2 (2, 3) more times—48 (52, 56) sts.

Rep sc row until work measures 1 row less than Right Half at beg of waist shaping, ending RS row.

Waist Shaping

Work waist rows 1–6 as for right half, without fastening off.

Work sc row once. Fasten off.

WAISTBAND

Join center back seam and center front seam down to markers. With shirring elastic doubled, make 2 rings to fit comfortably around waist, knotting each ring securely and leaving ends at least 2" long. With RS facing and size 3.00 mm hook, join yarn at top of center back seam.

Round 1: ch 1, *1 sc over first elastic ring and into next sc, rep from *, ending 1 sl st in first sc of round. (Work over ends of knot at the same time.)

Round 2: ch 1, 1 sc in each sc, ending 1 sl st in first sc of round.

Rep round 2 once more.

Rep round 1 working over second elastic ring. Fasten off.

LEG AND ANKLE BORDER

With RS facing and size 3.00 mm hook, join yarn at base of center back seam.

Round 1: ch 1, *1 sc in side edge of each row of leg to corner, 3 sc in same place at corner, work along ankle edge in base of ch: 1 sc in next sc, [sc2tog over next 2 sc, 1 sc in next sc] 14 (15, 16) times, 1 sc in each sc to corner, 3 sc in same place at corner, 1 sc in side edge of each row to center front seam, rep from * once more, ending at center back seam, 1 sl st in first sc of round.

Round 2: ch 1, 1 sc in first sc, 1 sc in each sc and 3 sc in second of 3 sc at each corner, ending skip last sc, 1 sl st in first sc of round. Rep round 2 a total of 3 more times. Fasten off.

Place front of border over back. Sew 1 snap to fasten at center, 1 at each ankle, and 2 (2, 3) more on each leg, evenly spaced.

Press as instructed on yarn labels

BOOTIES INSTRUCTIONS (make 2)

Begin at ankle: with size 3.50 mm hook, ch 27 (32, 37).

Row 1 (WS row): 1 sc in second ch from hook, 1 sc in each ch to end, turn—26 (31, 36) sc.

Sc row: ch 1, 1 sc in first sc, 1 sc in each sc to end, turn.

Rep sc row a total of 2 (2, 4) more times—4 (4, 6) rows.

TOP OF FOOT

Row 1 (WS row): ch 1, 1 sc in first sc, 1 sc in each of next 16 (19, 22) sc, turn.

Row 2: ch 1, 1 sc in first sc, 1 sc in each of next 7 (8, 9) sc, turn—8 (9, 10) sc.

Work 5 (7, 9) sc rows on these 8 (9, 10) sts.

Next row: ch 1, sc2tog over first 2 sc, 1 sc in each sc to last 2 sc, sc2tog, turn.

Rep this row once more—4 (5, 6) sts. Fasten off.

SIDES OF FOOT

With WS facing, rejoin yarn at turn of row 1 of foot, ch 1, 1 sc in each of 9 (11, 13) sc to end, turn.

Row 1: ch 1, 1 sc in each of next 9 (11, 13) sc, work 9 (11, 13) sc up side edge of foot, 4 (5, 6) sc across toe, 9 (11, 13) sc down side edge of foot and 1 sc in each of next 9 (11, 13) sc remaining from row 2, turn—40 (49, 58) sc.

Work sc row a total of 3 times.

Dec row 1: ch 1, 1 sc in first sc, 1 sc in each of next 15 (19, 23) sc, sc2tog over next 2 sc, 1 sc in each of next 4 (5, 6) sc, sc2tog over next 2 sc, 1 sc in each of next 16 (20, 24) sc to end, turn—38 (47, 56) sc.

Dec row 2: ch 1, sc2tog over first 2 sc, 1 sc in each st to last 2 sc, sc2tog, turn—36 (45, 54) sc.

Dec row 3: ch 1, 1 sc in first st, 1 sc in each of next 14 (18, 22) sc, sc2tog over next 2 sc, 1 sc in each of 2 (3, 4) sc, sc2tog over next 2 sc, 1 sc in each of 15 (19, 23) sts to end, turn—34 (43, 52) sc.

Dec row 4: as dec row 2—32 (41, 50) sc.

Second and Third Sizes Only

Dec row 5: ch 1, 1 sc in first st, 1 sc in each of next (17, 21) sc, sc2tog over next 2 sc, 1 sc in each of next (1, 2) sc, sc2tog over next 2 sc, 1 sc in each of next (18, 22) sts to end, turn—(39, 48) sc.

Third Size Only

Dec row 6: work as for dec row 2.

All Sizes

32 (39, 46) sts. Fasten off.

Fold last row in half and join with a flat seam. Join side edges of rows to form heel seam.

ANKLE CUFF

With RS facing and size 3.00 mm hook, join yarn at top of heel seam.

Round 1: ch 1, 1 sc in base of each sc, ending 1 sc in first sc of round.

Round 2: 1 sc in each sc all round.

Rep round 2 a total of 4 (5, 6) more times, ending at center back.

Change to size 3.50 mm hook and rep round 2 a total of 4 (5, 6) more times, ending at center back. Fasten off.

LACY JACKET

THIS COMFORTABLE-TO-WEAR JACKET HAS A CIRCULAR YOKE
AND NO SIDE OR SHOULDER SEAMS.

SIZES (see also page 26)

APPROXIMATE AGES	1–2 mos	2–3 mos	3–6 mos
to fit chest	14"	16"	18"
actual measurement	17¼"	19¼"	21"
length to shoulder	9"	10¼"	11½"
sleeve seam	4½"	5¼"	6½"

MATERIALS

2 (2, 2) balls of Snuggly 4-ply by Sirdar (55% nylon, 45%
acrylic, 50g/249yds), col 213 Angelica *or* comparable yarn
5 (5, 6) buttons
3.50 mm and 3.00 mm hooks

GAUGE

8½ patterns and 14 rows = 4" in speedwell stitch with size
3.50 mm hook
19 sts and 23 rows = 4" in rows of sc with size 3.50 mm
hook

Special Abbreviation: 1 dble dec sc2tog worked over
next and foll alt st as follows: insert hook in next st, yo,
pull through a lp, skip 1 st, insert hook in next st, yo, pull
through a lp, yo, pull through 3 lps on hook.

INSTRUCTIONS

BODY (made in 1 piece to armholes)
With size 3.50 mm hook, ch 111 (123, 135).
Foundation row (WS row): [1 hdc, ch 1, 1 hdc] in fourth ch from hook, *skip 2 ch, [1 hdc, ch 1, 1 hdc] in next ch, rep from * to last 2 ch, skip 1 ch, 1 hdc in next ch, turn—36 (40, 44) patts.
Patt row (speedwell stitch): ch 2, [1 hdc, ch 1, 1 hdc] in each ch-1 sp, ending 1 hdc under ch 2 at beg previous row, turn.
Rep this row until body measures 5½ (6¼, 7)", ending WS row.
Fasten off.

SPEEDWELL STITCH

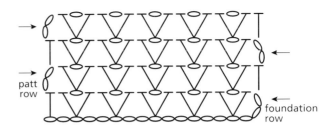

patt row

foundation row

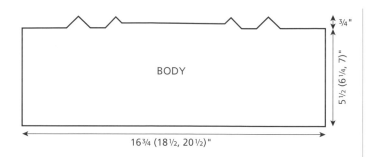

BODY

16¾ (18½, 20½)"

5½ (6¼, 7)"

¾"

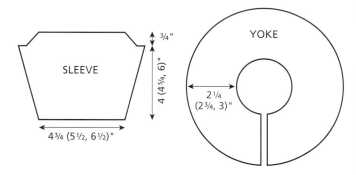

SLEEVE

4¾ (5½, 6½)"

¾"

4 (4¾, 6)"

YOKE

2¼ (2¾, 3)"

Left Front Shaping

With RS of body facing, leave first 3 (4, 5) patts, rejoin yarn to ch-1 sp at center of next patt.

**Dec row 1: ch 2, *[1 hdc, ch 1, 1 hdc] in next ch-1 sp, rep from * twice more, 1 hdc in next ch-1 sp, turn.

Dec row 2: ch 2, 1 hdc in first ch-1 sp, [1 hdc, ch 1, 1 hdc] in next ch-1 sp, hdc2tog over next ch-1 sp and second ch of ch 2 at beg previous row, turn.

Dec row 3: ch 2, hdc2tog over first ch-1 sp and second ch of ch 2 at beg previous row. Fasten off. **

Back Shaping

With RS of body facing, leave 2 whole patts along top edge after left front shaping, rejoin yarn to ch-1 sp at center of next patt.

Dec row 1: ch 2, *[1 hdc, ch 1, 1 hdc] in next ch-1 sp, rep from * 13 (15, 17) times, 1 hdc in next ch-1 sp, turn.

Dec row 2: ch 2, 1 hdc in first ch-1 sp, *[1 hdc, ch 1, 1 hdc] in next ch-1 sp, rep from * 11 (13, 15) times, hdc2tog over next ch-1 sp and second ch of ch 2, turn.

First Side

Dec row 3: ch 2, hdc2tog over first 2 ch-1 sps. Fasten off.

Second Side

With RS of body facing, leave 8 (10, 12) whole patts along top edge of body, rejoin yarn to center of next patt, ch 2, hdc2tog over center of next patt and second ch of ch 2. Fasten off.

Right Front Shaping

With RS of body facing, leave 2 whole patts along top edge after back shaping, rejoin yarn to ch-1 sp at center of next patt. Work as for left front from ** to **.

SLEEVES (make 2)

With size 3.50 mm hook, ch 33 (39, 45).
Work foundation row and patt row as for body—10 (12, 14) patts. Rep patt row 0 (1, 2) more times—2 (3, 4) rows.

Inc row 1: ch 3, 1 hdc in first hdc, work patt as set, ending [1 hdc, ch 1, 1 hdc] in second ch of ch 2 at beg previous row, turn.

Inc row 2: ch 3, 1 hdc in first ch-1 sp, work patt as set, ending [1 hdc, ch 1, 1 hdc] under ch 3 at beg previous row, turn.

Inc row 3: ch 2, [1 hdc, ch 1, 1 hdc] in first ch-1 sp and each ch-1 sp, ending [1 hdc, ch 1, 1 hdc] under ch 3 at beg previous row, 1 hdc in second ch of ch 3, turn.

Inc row 4: work as for patt row—12 (14, 16) patts; 6 (7, 8) rows.
Rep inc rows 1–4 twice more—16 (18, 20) patts; 14 (15, 16) rows.
Rep patt row until sleeve measures 4 (4¾, 6)" in all, ending WS row.

Top of Sleeve Shaping

Dec row 1: sl st across [2 hdc, ch 1] twice, ch 2, work 12 (14, 16) patts as set, 1 hdc in next ch-1 sp, turn.

Dec row 2: ch 2, 1 hdc in first ch-1 sp, work 10 (12, 14) patts as set, hdc2tog over last ch-1 sp and second ch of ch 2, turn.

Dec row 3: ch 2, 1 hdc in first ch-1 sp, work 8 (10, 12) patts as set, hdc2tog over last ch-1 sp and second ch of ch 2. Fasten off.

YOKE

Join sleeve seams. Join sleeves to body at each armhole, matching shaping rows.

With RS facing and size 3.50 mm hook, join yarn at top of right front edge.

Row 1: ch 1, 16 (19, 22) sc along neck edge to seam, 29 (32, 35) sc across top of first sleeve, 30 (36, 42) sc across top of back, 29 (32, 35) sc across top of second sleeve, 16 (19, 22) sc along left front neck edge to end, turn—120 (138, 156) sc.

Row 2: ch 1, 1 sc in first sc, 1 sc in each of next 3 (7, 9) sc, [sc2tog over next 2 sc, 1 sc in each of next 8 (6, 5) sc] 11 (15, 19) times, sc2tog over next 2 sc, 1 sc in each of 4 (8, 11) sc to end, turn—108 (122, 136) sts.

Row 3: ch 1, 1 sc in first sc, 1 sc in each st to end, turn.

Row 4: work as for row 3.

Row 5: ch 1, sc2tog over first 2 sc, 1 sc in each of next 10 (8, 6) sc, [1 dble dec, 1 sc in each of next 6 (8, 10) sc] 9 times, 1 dble dec, 1 sc in each of next 10 (8, 6) sc, sc2tog over last 2 sc, turn—86 (100, 114) sts.

Rows 6–8: work as for row 3.

Row 9: ch 1, sc2tog over first 2 sc, 1 sc in each of next 8 (6, 4) sc, [1 dble dec, 1 sc in each of next 4 (6, 8) sc] 9 times, 1 dble dec, 1 sc in each of next 8 (6, 4) sc, sc2tog over last 2 sc, turn—64 (78, 92) sts.

Rows 10–12: work as for row 3.

Row 13: ch 1, sc2tog over first 2 sc, 1 sc in each of next 6 (4, 2) sc, [1 dble dec, 1 sc in each of next 2 (4, 6) sc] 9 times, 1 dble dec,1 sc in each of next 6 (4, 2) sc, sc2tog over last 2 sc, turn—42 (56, 70) sts.

Row 14: work as for row 3.

First Size Only

Fasten off.

Second Size Only

Row 15: ch 1, sc2tog over first 2 sc, 1 sc in each of next 5 sc, [sc2tog over next 2 sc, 1 sc in each of next 6 sc] 5 times, sc2tog over next 2 sc, 1 sc in each of next 5 sc, sc2tog over last 2 sc, turn—48 sts.

Row 16: work as for row 3. Fasten off.

Third Size Only

Row 15: ch 1, sc2tog over first 2 sc, 1 sc in each of next 7 sc, [sc2tog over next 2 sc, 1 sc in each of next 8 sc] 5 times, sc2tog over next 2 sc, 1 sc in each of next 7 sc, sc2tog over last 2 sc, turn—62 sts.

Row 16: work as for row 3.

Row 17: ch 1, sc2tog over first 2 sc, 1 sc in each of next 3 sc, [sc2tog over next 2 sc, 1 sc in each of next 8 sc] 5 times, sc2tog over next 2 sc, 1 sc in each of next 3 sc, sc2tog over last 2 sc, turn—54 sts.

Row 18: work as for row 3. Fasten off.

FINISHING

Cuffs (make 2)

With RS facing and size 3.00 mm hook, join yarn at base of sleeve seam.

Round 1: ch 1, 1 sc in first ch sp, 2 sc in each ch sp, ending 1 sc in last ch sp, 1 sl st in first sc of round.

Round 2: ch 1, 1 sc in first sc, *ch 2, 1 sc in each of next 2 sc, rep from *, ending 1 sl st in first sc of round. Fasten off.

Front, Neck, and Lower Border

With RS facing and size 3.00 mm hook, join yarn to 1 ch-2 sp on lower edge below 1 sleeve.

Round 1: ch 1, 1 sc in same ch sp, 2 sc in each ch sp, ending 1 sc in last ch sp at corner, 3 sc in same place at corner, 42 (48, 54) sc evenly spaced up right front edge, 3 sc in same place at corner, 1 sc in each sc around neck to top of left front edge, 3 sc in same place at corner, 42 (48, 54) sc evenly spaced down left front edge, 3 sc in same place at corner and 2 sc in each ch sp along lower edge, ending 1 sl st in first sc of round.

To button right front over left: round 2: ch 1, 1 sc in first sc, 1 sc in each sc to corner, 3 sc in second of 3 sc at corner, 1 sc in each of next 9 (15, 13) sc of right front edge, [ch 2, skip 2 sc, 1 sc in each of next 6 sc] 4 (4, 5) times, ch 2, skip 2 sc, *1 sc in each sc to corner, 3 sc in same place at corner, rep from * all around, ending 1 sl st in first sc of round.

Round 3: ch 1, 1 sc in first sc, *ch 2, 1 sc in each of next 2 sc*, rep from * to * to corner, [ch 2, 2 sc] in second of 3 sc at corner, 1 sc in each sc and 2 sc in each ch sp up right front edge to corner, [ch 2, 2 sc] in second of 3 sc at corner, rep from * to * along neck edge, ending [ch 2, 2 sc] in second of 3 sc at corner, 1 sc in each sc down left front edge to corner, [ch 2, 2 sc] in second of 3 sc at corner, rep from * to * along lower edge, ending 1 sl st in first sc of round. Fasten off.

(To button left front over right: round 2: work as for round 2 of right front over left, but on right front edge work 1 sc in each sc, and on left front edge work 1 sc in first sc, rep [to] 4 (4, 5) times, ch 2, skip 2 sc, complete as given.

Round 3: work as for round 3 above, working 1 sc in each sc on front edges, and 2 sc in each ch-2 sp on left front edge. Fasten off.)

Sew on buttons to match buttonholes.

Press as instructed on yarn labels.

This delightful blue alternative has been crocheted in Snuggly 4-ply by Sirdar in col 216 Sky.

TWO EASY PULLOVERS

ONE BASIC PATTERN WITH A CHOICE OF TRIMS AND EDGINGS.

SIZES (see also page 30)

APPROXIMATE AGES	2–3 mos	3–6 mos	6–12 mos
to fit chest	16"	18"	20"
actual measurement	18"	20"	22"
length to shoulder	9¾"	11"	11¾"
sleeve seam	6"	6¾"	8"

MATERIALS

LITTLE FLOWERS PULLOVER
2 (3, 3) balls of Peter Pan DK by Wendy (55% nylon, 45% acrylic, 50g/180yds), col A (300 Pure White) *or comparable yarn*
Small ball of Peter Pan DK by Wendy, col B (336 Delphinium) or comparable weight yarn
4.00 mm and 3.50 mm hooks
4 buttons

STRAWBERRY PULLOVER
2 (3, 3) balls of Peter Pan DK by Wendy (55% nylon, 45% acrylic, 50g/180yds), col A (301 Spring Lamb)
Small ball of Peter Pan DK by Wendy, col B (311 Miss Muffet)
Small amount of Peter Pan DK by Wendy, col C (309 Leprechaun)
4.00 mm and 3.50 mm hooks
4 buttons

GAUGE

16½ sts and 19 rows = 4" in sc with size 4.00 mm hook

SINGLE CROCHET ROWS

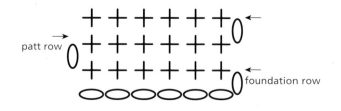

LITTLE FLOWERS PULLOVER INSTRUCTIONS

BACK
With size 4.00 mm hook and col A, ch 39 (43, 47).
Foundation row: 1 sc in second ch from hook, 1 sc in each ch to end, turn—38 (42, 46) sc.
Patt row: ch 1, 1 sc in first sc, 1 sc in each sc to end, turn.*
Rep patt row until back measures 8¾" (10, 10¾)", ending with a WS row.

Button Border
First Side
Change to size 3.50 mm hook.
Row 1: ch 1, 1 sc in first sc, 1 sc in each of next 10 (11, 12) sc, turn.
Work 3 more patt rows on these 11 (12, 13) sts. Fasten off.
Second Side
With RS of back facing and size 3.50 mm hook, leave 16 (18, 20) sc at center back and rejoin col A to next sc.
Row 1: ch 1, 1 sc in same sc, 1 sc in each of 10 (11, 12) sc to end, turn.
Work 3 more rows of sc on these 11 (12, 13) sts. Fasten off.

FRONT
Work as given for back to *.
Rep patt row until front measures 8 (8, 10) rows less than back to beg of button border, ending with a WS row.

Front Neck Shaping
First Side
Row 1: ch 1, 1 sc in first sc, 1 sc in each of next 12 (13, 14) sc, sc2tog over next 2 sc, turn.
Row 2: ch 1, skip sc2tog, 1 sc in each of next 13 (14, 15) sc, turn.
Row 3: ch 1, 1 sc in first sc, 1 sc in each of next 10 (11, 12) sc, sc2tog over next 2 sc, turn.
Row 4: ch 1, skip sc2tog, 1 sc in each of next 11 (12, 13) sc, turn.
Work 4 (4, 6) more rows of sc on these 11 (12, 13) sts.

Buttonhole Band
Change to size 3.50 mm hook.
Work 2 more rows.
Buttonhole row: ch 1, 1 sc in first sc, 1 sc in each of next 2 sc, ch 2, skip 2 sc, 1 sc in each of next 3 (4, 5) sc, ch 2, skip 2 sc, 1 sc in last sc, turn.
Foll row: ch 1, 1 sc in first sc, 1 sc in each sc and 2 sc in each ch-2 sp to end. Fasten off.
Second Side
With RS of front facing and size 4.00 mm hook, leave 8 (10, 12) sts at center front and rejoin col A to next sc.
Row 1: ch 1, 1 sc in foll sc, 1 sc in each of next 13 (14, 15) sc to end, turn.
Row 2: ch 1, 1 sc in first sc, 1 sc in each of next 11 (12, 13) sc, sc2tog over last 2 sc, turn.

Row 3: ch 1, skip sc2tog, 1 sc in each of next 12 (13, 14) sc to end, turn.

Row 4: ch 1, 1 sc in first sc, 1 sc in each of next 9 (10, 11) sc, sc2tog over last 2 sc, turn.

Row 5: ch 1, 1 sc in sc2tog, 1 sc in each of next 10 (11, 12) sc to end, turn.

Work 3 (3, 5) more rows on these 11 (12, 13) sts.

Buttonhole Band

Change to size 3.50 mm hook.

Work 2 more rows.

Buttonhole row: ch 1, 1 sc in first sc, ch 2, skip 2 sc, 1 sc in each of next 3 (4, 5) sc, ch 2, skip 2 sc, 1 sc in each of next 3 sc to end, turn.

Foll row: ch 1, 1 sc in first sc, 1 sc in each sc and 2 sc in each ch-2 sp to end. Fasten off.

SLEEVES (make 2)

Place buttonhole border over button border at each shoulder and stitch together at armhole edges. From base of each border count 22 (25, 28) rows down back or front and place a marker on side edge.

Row 1: with RS facing, size 4.00 mm hook, and col A, work 37 (41, 45) sc evenly along armhole edge between markers, working through both thicknesses at shoulder (spacing is about 3 sts to every 4 rows), turn.

Patt row: ch 1, 1 sc in first sc, 1 sc in each sc to end, turn.

Rep patt row 0 (2, 4) more times—2 (4, 6) rows in all.

Dec row 1: ch 1, skip first sc, 1 sc in each sc to end, turn.

Dec row 2: work as for dec row 1.

Dec rows 3 and 4: work as for patt row—35 (39, 43) sts; 6 (8, 10) rows in all.

Rep these 4 rows a total of 4 (4, 5) more times—27 (31, 33) sts; 22 (24, 30) rows in all.

Rep patt row until sleeve measures 5½ (6¼, 7½)" or length required minus ½". Fasten off.

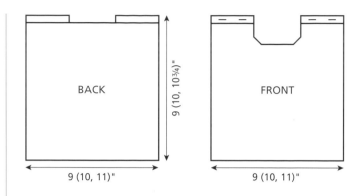

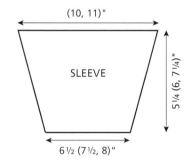

FINISHING

Join side and sleeve seams by slip stitching on WS, matching row ends.

Cuffs (make 2)

With RS facing, size 3.50 mm hook, and col A, join yarn to 1 sc at sleeve seam.

Scallop Border

Round 1: ch 1, 1 sc in first sc, 1 sc in each sc, ending 1 sc under ch 1 at beg of round—27 (31, 33) sc.

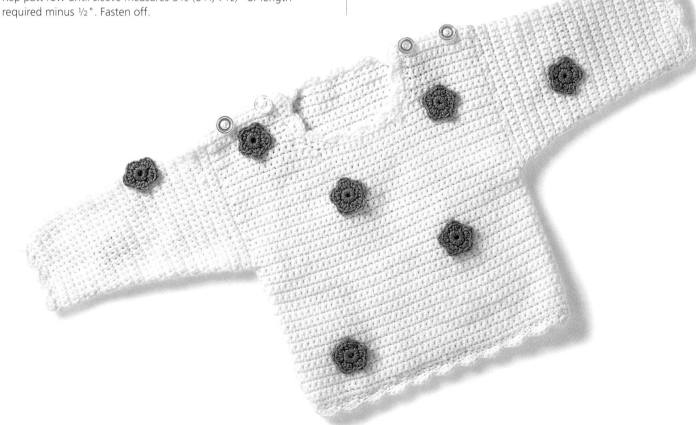

Round 2: ch 1, 1 sc in first sc, 1 sc in each sc, working sc2tog 3 (3, 5) times evenly spaced, ending 1 sl st in 1 sc at beg of round—24 (28, 28) sts.

Round 3: skip first sc, *4 hdc in next sc, skip 1 sc, 1 sl st in next sc, skip 1 sc, rep from *, ending 1 sl st in last sc, 1 sl st in first hdc at beg of round—6 (7, 7) patts. Fasten off.

Lower Border
With RS facing, size 3.50 mm hook, and col A, join yarn to base of ch 1 at 1 side seam.
Round 1: work as for round 1 of cuff—76 (84, 92) sc.
Round 2: ch 1, 1 sc in first sc, 1 sc in each sc, ending 1 sl st in first sc of round.
Round 3: work as for round 3 of cuff. Fasten off.

Back Neck Border
With RS facing, size 3.50 mm hook, and col A, join yarn to corner of first side button border.
Row 1: ch 1, work 19 (23, 25) sc evenly spaced along back neck edge, turn.
Row 2: ch 1, 1 sc in first sc, 1 sc in each sc, working sc2tog 2 (2, 4) times evenly spaced, turn—17 (21, 21) sc.
Row 3: skip first 2 sc, *4 hdc in next sc, skip next sc, 1 sl st in next sc, skip next sc, rep from *, ending 1 sl st in last sc—4 (5, 5) patts. Fasten off.

Front Neck Border
With RS facing, size 3.50 mm hook, and col A, join yarn to corner of first side buttonhole band.
Row 1: ch 1, work 32 (36, 40) sc evenly along neck edge.
Row 2: ch 1, 1 sc in first sc, 1 sc in each sc, working sc2tog 3 times evenly spaced, turn—29 (33, 37) sc.
Row 3: work as for row 3 of back neck border—7 (8, 9) patts. Fasten off.
Sew on buttons to match buttonholes.
Press as instructed on yarn labels.

Flower Trim (make about 14)
Round 1: with size 3.50 mm hook and col B, ch 5 and join into a ring with 1 sl st in first ch made.
Round 2: (work over starting end of yarn) ch 1, 10 sc into ring, 1 sl st in first sc of round.
Round 3: *[1 hdc, 1 dc, 1hdc] in next sc, 1 sl st in next sc, rep from * 4 more times. Fasten off, leaving yarn end about 10". Pull gently on starting end of yarn to tighten center.
Arrange flowers on pullover following the photograph as a guide. Sew in place with long yarn ends.
Press as instructed on yarn labels.

FLOWER TRIM

STRAWBERRY PULLOVER INSTRUCTIONS

BACK, FRONT, AND SLEEVES
Work in col A as given for Little Flowers Pullover.

FINISHING
Join side and sleeve seams by slip stitching on WS, matching row ends.
Cuffs (make 2)
With RS facing, size 3.50 mm hook, and col A, join yarn to 1 sc at sleeve seam.
Loop Border
Round 1: ch 1, 1 sc in base of each sc, ending 1 sc under ch 1 at beg of round—27 (31, 33) sc.
Round 2: ch 1, 1 sc in first sc, 1 sc in each sc, working sc2tog 5 times evenly spaced, ending 1 sl st in 1 sc at beg of round—22 (26, 28) sts.
Round 3: ch 3, skip 1 sc at base of ch 3, *1 sl st in next sc, 1 sc in next sc, ch 2, rep from *, ending 1 sl st in first ch of ch 3 at beg of round—11 (13, 14) patts. Fasten off.

Lower Border
With RS facing, size 3.50 mm hook, and col A, join yarn to base of ch 1 at one side seam.
Round 1: work as for round 1 of cuff—76 (84, 92) sc.
Round 2: ch 1, 1 sc in first sc, 1 sc in each sc ending, 1 sl st in first sc of round.
Round 3: work as for round 3 of cuff. Fasten off.

Back Neck Border
With RS facing, size 3.50 mm hook, and col A, join yarn to corner of first side button border.
Row 1: ch 1, work 19 (21, 23) sc evenly spaced along back neck edge, turn.
Row 2: ch 1, 1 sc in first sc, 1 sc in each sc, working sc2tog 3 times evenly spaced, turn—16 (18, 20) sc.

STRAWBERRY MOTIF

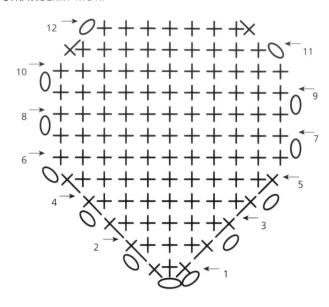

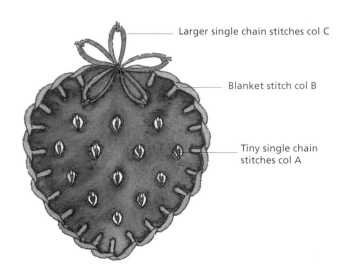

Larger single chain stitches col C

Blanket stitch col B

Tiny single chain stitches col A

Row 3: skip first sc, *ch 2, 1 sl st in next sc, 1 sc in next sc, rep from *, ending 1 sl st in last sc—8 (9, 10) patts. Fasten off.

Front Neck Border
With RS facing, size 3.50 mm hook, and col A, join yarn to corner of first side buttonhole band.
Row 1: ch 1, work 32 (36, 40) sc evenly along neck edge, turn.
Row 2: ch 1, 1 sc in first sc, 1 sc in each sc, working sc2tog twice evenly spaced, turn—30 (34, 38) sc.
Row 3: work as for row 3 of back neck border—15 (17, 19) patts. Fasten off.
Sew on buttons to match buttonholes.
Press as instructed on yarn labels.

Strawberry Motif
With size 3.50 mm hook, and col B, ch 2.
Row 1: 3 sc in second ch from hook, turn.
Row 2: ch 1, 2 sc in first sc, 1 sc in next sc, 2 sc in last sc, turn—5 sc.
Row 3: ch 1, 2 sc in first sc, 1 sc in each of next 3 sc, 2 sc in last sc, turn—7 sc.
Row 4: ch 1, 2 sc in first sc, 1 sc in each of next 5 sc, 2 sc in last sc, turn—9 sc.
Row 5: ch 1, 2 sc in first sc, 1 sc in each of next 7 sc, 2 sc in last sc, turn—11 sc.
Row 6: ch 1, 1 sc in first sc, 1 sc in each of next 10 sc, turn.

Rows 7, 8, 9, and 10: work as for row 6.
Row 11: ch 1, skip first sc, 1 sc in each of next 8 sc, sc2tog over last 2 sc, turn—9 sts.
Row 12: ch 1, skip sc2tog, 1 sc in each of next 6 sc, sc2tog over last 2 sc—7 sts. Fasten off.
Sew motif to center front, about 2 " below neck edge, using col B to work all around in blanket stitch as shown in embroidery diagram. Use col A to work tiny single chain stitches to represent seeds, and col C to work larger chain stitches for leaves, as shown.
See page 12 for diagrams of these embroidery stitches.
Press as instructed on yarn labels.

STRIPED PULLOVER WITH TOY RABBIT

**SIMPLE TO MAKE AND EASY TO WEAR, THIS PULLOVER HAS
A POCKET THAT'S JUST THE RIGHT SIZE FOR A TOY RABBIT.**

STRIPED PULLOVER

SIZES

APPROXIMATE AGES	6–12 mos	1–2 yrs	3–4 yrs
to fit chest	20"	22"	24"
actual measurement	22½"	24½"	26½"
length to shoulder	14"	15½"	17¼"
sleeve seam	8"	9½"	11"

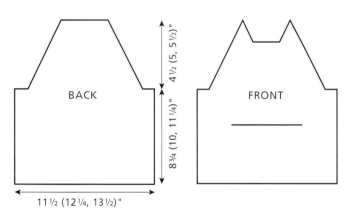

BACK

4½ (5, 5½)"

8¾ (10, 11¼)"

11½ (12¼, 13½)"

FRONT

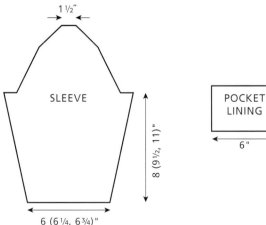

1½"

SLEEVE

POCKET LINING

4½"

6"

8 (9½, 11)"

6 (6¼, 6¾)"

MATERIALS

2 (3, 3) balls of Calypso DK by Sirdar (100% cotton,
50g/116yds), col A (670 White) *or* comparable yarn
2 (3, 3) balls of Calypso DK by Sirdar, col B (689 Azure Blue)
or comparable yarn
4.00 mm and 3.50 mm hooks
3 buttons

GAUGE

16 sts and 17½ rows = 4" in stripe pattern with size 4.00
mm hook

Special Abbreviation: scf sc in front lp only of st below.

NOTE
When working in stripes, change cols as follows: at the
end of second and every alt row, work the last yo and pull
through in the col required for the foll row.

INSTRUCTIONS

BACK
With size 4.00 mm hook and col A, ch 47 (51, 55).
Foundation row: 1 sc in second ch from hook, 1 sc in each ch to end,
turn—46 (50, 54) sc.
Next row: ch 1, 1 sc in each sc to end, changing to col B for last yo, turn.
Stripe Pattern
Row 1: (with col B) ch 1, 1 scf in each sc to end, turn.
Row 2: ch 1, 1 sc in each scf to end, changing to col A at end of row,
turn.
Row 3: (with col A) work as for row 1.
Row 4: work as for row 3, changing to col B at end of row, turn.
These 4 rows form the stripe pattern.*
Rep them 8 (9, 11) more times.

STRIPE PATTERN

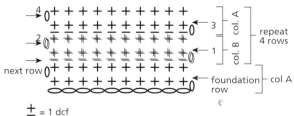

± = 1 dcf

Second Size Only
Work rows 1 and 2 once more.
All Sizes
38 (44, 50) rows in all, ending 2 rows col A (B, A).
Raglan Armhole Shaping
**Cont throughout in stripe pattern as set:
Dec row 1: sl st across first 4 sts, ch 1, 1 scf in each sc to last 3 sc, turn, leaving last 3 sts unworked.
Dec row 2: ch 1, 1 sc in each scf, ending 1 sc in ch 1 at beg dec row 1, turn—40 (44, 48) sts.
Dec row 3: ch 1, skip first sc, 1 scf in each sc to end, leaving ch 1 at beg previous row unworked, turn.
Dec row 4: ch 1, skip first scf, 1 sc in each scf to end, leaving ch 1 at beg previous row unworked, turn—38 (42, 46) sts. **
Rep dec rows 3 and 4 a total of 8 (9, 10) more times, ending 2 rows col A—22 (24, 26) sts.
Fasten off.

POCKET LINING
With size 4.00 mm hook and col A, ch 25.
Work foundation row as for back—24 sc.
Work foll row as for back.
Rep stripe pattern rows 1–4 as for back 4 times in all, and rows 1 and 2 once again—20 rows in all, ending 2 rows col B. Fasten off.

FRONT
Work as given for back to *.
Rep the 4 stripe pattern rows a total of 5 (6, 7) more times, and rows 1 and 2 once again—28 (32, 36) rows, ending 2 rows col B.
Pocket Lining Placement
Next row: (with col A) ch 1, 1 scf in each of next 11 (13, 15) sc, then work across top edge of pocket lining: with RS facing, 1 scf in each of next 24 sc; skip next 24 sc at center of front, 1 scf in each of 11 (13, 15) sc to end, turn.
Work 9 (11, 13) more rows stripe pattern—38 (44, 50) rows in all, ending 2 rows col A (B, A).
Raglan Armhole Shaping
Work as given for back from ** to **.
Rep dec rows 3 and 4 a total of 4 (5, 6) more times—30 (32, 34) sts, ending 2 rows col A.
Front Neck Shaping
First Side
Neck row 1: ch 1, skip 1 sc, 1 scf in each of next 8 sc, turn.
Neck row 2: ch 1, skip 1 scf, 1 sc in each scf to end, turn.
Neck row 3: ch 1, skip 1 sc, 1 scf in each sc to end, turn.
Rep neck rows 2 and 3 twice more—2 sts.
Neck row 8: ch 1, skip 1 scf, 1 sc in last scf. Fasten off.
Second Side
With RS front facing, leave 12 (14, 16) sc at center front and rejoin col B to next sc, ch 1, 1 scf in each of next 8 sc to end.
Work neck rows 2–8 as for first side. Fasten off.

SLEEVES (make 2)
With size 4.00 mm hook and col A, ch 25 (27, 29).
Work foundation row and foll row as given for back—24 (26, 28) sts.
Inc row 1: (with col B), ch 1, 2 scf in first sc, 1 scf in each sc to end, turn.
Inc row 2: ch 1, 2 sc in first scf, 1 sc in each scf to end, turn.
Inc rows 3 and 4: (using col A) work as for stripe pattern—26 (28, 30) sts.
Rep these 4 rows a total of 6 (7, 8) more times—38 (42, 46) sts; 30 (34, 38) rows in all.

Work 4 (6, 12) more rows stripe pattern—34 (40, 50) rows in all, ending 2 rows col A (B, A).

Raglan Sleeve Shaping

Work ** to ** as given for back—30 (34, 38) sts.

Rep dec rows 3 and 4 a total of 4 more times—22 (26, 30) sts.

Next dec row: ch 1, skip first st, 1 scf in each sc to last 2 sts, 2scftog over last 2 sts, turn.

Foll dec row: ch 1, skip first st, 1 sc in each scf to last 2 sts, sc2tog over last 2 sts, turn—18 (22, 26) sts.

Rep these 2 rows a total of 3 (4, 5) more times—6 sts rem. Fasten off.

FINISHING

Join raglan seams by sl st on WS, matching row ends, and leaving an opening of 12 rows (6 stripes) at top of right rront raglan seam.

Join side and sleeve seams. Sew down pocket lining to WS of front, matching stripes.

Cuffs (make 2)

With RS facing and size 3.50 mm hook, join col B to base of ch 1 at sleeve seam.

Round 1: ch 1, 1 sc in base of each ch, ending 1 sc under ch 1 at beg of round.

Round 2: ch 3, *1 sl st in each of next 2 sc, ch 2, rep from *, ending 1 sl st in first of ch 3 at beg of round. Fasten off.

Lower Border

With RS facing and size 3.50 mm hook, join col B to base of ch 1 at one side seam. Work rounds 1 and 2 as for cuff. Fasten off.

Neck Border

With RS facing and size 3.50 mm hook, join col B to top of right sleeve.

Row 1: ch 1, 1 sc in each sc across top of right sleeve, back neck and top of left sleeve, 8 sc down side edge of front neck shaping, 12 (14, 16) sc across center front and 8 sc up side edge of front neck shaping, turn.

Row 2: ch 1, 1 sc in each sc to end, taking sc2tog at each of next 4 corners of neck edge, turn.

Row 3: ch 3, *1 sl st in each of next 2 sc, ch 2, rep from *, ending 1 sl st in last sc.

Do not fasten off but cont.

Front Edge of Opening

Row 1: ch 2, 2 sc in side edge of neck border rows, 2 sc in side edge of each of 6 stripes, turn—14 sc.

Row 2: ch 1, 1 sc in each of first 2 sc, [ch 2, skip 2 sc, 1 sc in each of next 3 sc] twice, ch 2, skip 2 sc, 1 sc in second ch of ch 2, turn.

Row 3: ch 1, 1 sc in each sc and 2 sc in each ch sp to end.

Fasten off.

Back Edge of Opening

With RS facing and size 3.50 mm hook, join col B to side edge of first row at base of opening.

Row 1: ch 1, 1 sc in side edge of next row, 2 sc in side edge of each stripe, 2 sc in side edge of neck border rows, turn—13 sc.

Row 2: ch 1, 1 sc in each sc to end. Fasten off.

Sew on buttons to match buttonholes.

Press as instructed on yarn labels.

TOY RABBIT

SIZE

height   approx. 6" excluding ears

MATERIALS

1 ball of Calypso DK by Sirdar (100% cotton,
50g/116yds), col A (676 Saffron) or comparable yarn
4.00 mm hook
Small amount of washable polyester stuffing
Small amount of black yarn
Darning needle

GAUGE

16 sts and 18 rows = 4" in rows of sc with size 4.00 mm
hook

INSTRUCTIONS

BACK

With size 4.00 mm hook and col A, ch 21.
*Row 1: 1 sc in second ch from hook, 1 sc in each ch to end, turn—20 sc.
Row 2: ch 1, 2 sc in first sc, 1 sc in each sc to last sc, 2 sc in last sc, turn—22 sc.
Row 3: work as for row 2—24 sc.
Row 4: ch 1, 1 sc in each sc to end, turn.
Row 5: ch 1, skip first sc, 1 sc in each sc to last 2 sc, sc2tog over last 2 sc, turn—22 sts. Rep this row a total of 4 more times—14 sts.
Rep row 4 a total of 3 more times—12 rows in all.
Row 13: work as for row 2—16 sc. Rep this row a total of 3 more times—22 sc.
Work row 4 twice more—18 rows in all. *

HEAD SHAPING

Row 19: 1 sl st in each of first 8 sc, ch 1, 1 sc in each of next 6 sc, turn.
Row 20: ch 1, 1 sc in each of 6 sc, turn.
Row 21: ch 1, 2 sc in first sc, 1 sc in next sc, [2 sc in next sc] twice, 1 sc in next sc, 2 sc in last sc, turn—10 sc.
Row 22: ch 1, 2 sc in first sc, 1 sc in each of next 3 sc, [2 sc in next sc] twice, 1 sc in each of next 3 sc, 2 sc in last sc, turn—14 sc.
Row 23: ch 1, 2 sc in first sc, 1 sc in each of next 5 sc, [2 sc in next sc] twice, 1 sc in each of next 5 sc, 2 sc in last sc, turn—18 sts.
Row 24: ch 1, 2 sc in first sc, 1 sc in each sc to last sc, 2 sc in last sc, turn. 20 sts.
Row 25: ch 1, 1 sc in each of next 5 sc, sc2tog, 1 sc in each of next 6 sc, sc2tog, 1 sc in each of next 5 sc to end, turn. 18 sts.
Row 26: ch 1, 1 sc in each of next 4 sc, sc2tog, 1 sc in each of next 6 sc, sc2tog, 1 sc in each of next 4 sc to end, turn—16 sts.
Row 27: ch 1, 1 sc in each of next 4 sc, sc2tog, 1 sc in each of next 4 sc, sc2tog, 1 sc in each of next 4 sc to end, turn—14 sts.
Row 28: ch 1, 2 sc in first sc, 1 sc in each of next 2 sc, [sc2tog] 4 times, 1 sc in each of next 2 sc, 2 sc in last sc, turn—12 sts.
Fold top edge in half and work a row of sl st through both edges together. Fasten off.

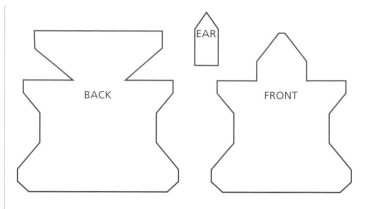

FRONT

With size 4.00 mm hook and col A, ch 17.
Work as given for back from * to *. Note that there will be 4 sts less than given throughout.

Chin Shaping
Row 19: 1 sl st in each of first 6 sc, ch 1, 1 sc in each of next 6 sc, turn.
Row 20: ch 1, 1 sc in each of 6 sc, turn.
Rep this row a total of 3 more times.
Row 24: ch 1, 1 sc in each of next 2 sc, sc2tog, 1 sc in each of last 2 sc, turn—5 sts.
Row 25: ch 1, 1 sc in each st to end, turn.
Row 26: ch 1, 1 sc in first sc, sc3tog, 1 sc in last sc, turn—3 sts.
Row 27: work as for row 25.
Row 28: ch 1, sc3tog. Fasten off.

EARS (make 2)

With size 4.00 mm hook and col A, ch 10.
Row 1: skip 3 ch, 1 dc in each of next 5 ch, 1 hdc in next ch, [1 sc, ch 1, 1 sc] in last ch, then cont along lower edge of ch: 1 hdc between hdc and next dc, [1 dc between next 2 dc] 4 times, 1 dc between last dc and ch 3 at beg of row 1. Fasten off, leaving about 8" end.

FINISHING

Matching point of chin to end of seam at top of back head, join side edges. Take in slight fullness along top of each arm. Leave lower edge open. Insert toy filling. With needle, slip stitch lower edges together, spreading fullness evenly. Sew ears to top of head, gathering slightly to help them stand up.

Double the black yarn and thread the loop through the darning needle. At one side of head, in position for eye, pass needle under one stitch and through the loop of black yarn to secure. Then pass the needle through the head to the corresponding position on the opposite side and pull gently to shape the head. Make a small backstitch. For the eye, make a French knot in the same place, and then pass the needle back through the head. Pull gently as before, make another backstitch and another French knot for the second eye. Run the needle inside the head through to the point of the nose and make about 4 straight stitches, fanned out from the point of the nose (see photograph). Secure with a backstitch and run the end inside the head.

ROSEBUD PULLOVER

THIS PULLOVER IS QUICK TO MAKE IN LIGHT YARN, WITH
BORDERS OF ROSEBUD MOTIFS.

SIZES (see also page 42)

APPROXIMATE AGES	2–3 mos	3–6 mos	6–12 mos
to fit chest	16"	18"	20"
actual measurement	18"	20"	21¾"
length to shoulder	9½"	10½"	11½"
sleeve seam	6"	6¾"	8"

INSTRUCTIONS

BACK
With size 4.50 mm hook, ch 40 (44, 48).

Rosebud Border

Row 1 (WS row): 1 dc in third ch from hook, 1 dc in each ch to
end, turn—39 (43, 47) sts.

Row 2: ch 2, skip first dc, 1 dc in each of next 4 (2, 4) dc, *skip 2
dc, dc3tog in next dc, inserting hook behind this dc3tog, work 1 dc
in each of 2 missed dc, 1 dc in same place as dc3tog, 1 dc in each
of next 2 dc, inserting hook into same place as base of dc3tog work
dc3tog, 1 dc in each of next 3 dc, rep from *, ending 1 dc in each of
4 (2, 4) dc, 1 dc in second ch of ch 2, turn—4 (5, 5) pairs of leaves.

ROSEBUD BORDER

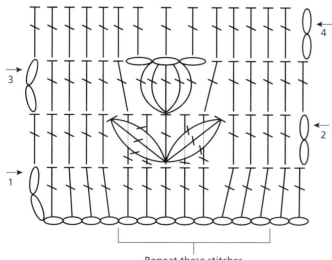

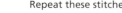
Repeat these stitches

 = 5 double crochet popcorn

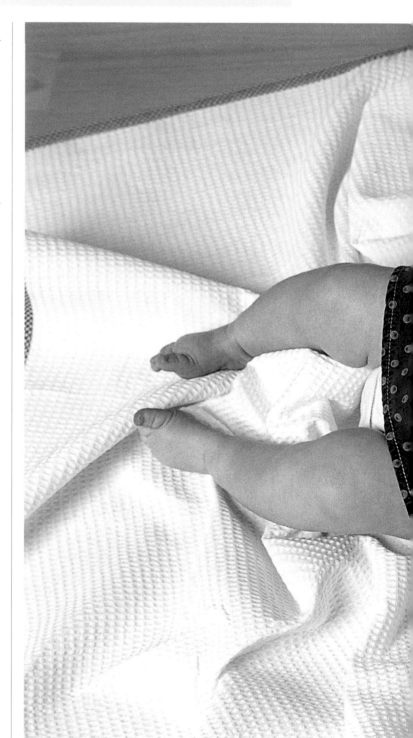

MATERIALS

2 (3, 3) balls of Peter Pan DK by Wendy (55% nylon, 45% acrylic, 50g/180yds), 317 Candy Pink *or* comparable yarn
4.50 mm and 4.00 mm hooks
4 buttons

GAUGE

8½ patts and 17 rows = 4" in bud stitch with size 4.50 mm hook

Special Abbreviation: 1 popcorn (worked on WS row) 5 dc in next dc, remove hook from working loop, insert hook through top of first of these 5 dc from back to front of work, catch working loop and pull it through, thus tightening top of popcorn and pushing it toward RS of work.

Row 3: ch 2, skip first dc, 1 dc in each of 4 (2, 4) dc, *skip top of dc3tog, 1 dc in next dc, ch 1, skip 1 dc, 1 popcorn in next dc, ch 1, skip 1 dc, 1 dc in next dc, skip top of dc3tog, 1 dc in each of next 3 dc, rep from *, ending 1 dc in each of 4 (2, 4) dc, 1 dc in second ch of ch 2, turn—4 (5, 5) motifs.

Row 4: ch 2, skip first dc, 1 dc in each of 5 (3, 5) dc, *1 dc in ch-1 sp, 1 dc in closing lp of popcorn, 1 dc in ch-1 sp, 1 dc in each of 5 dc, rep from *, ending 1 dc in each of 5 (3, 5) dc, 1 dc in second ch of ch 2, turn—39 (43, 47) sts.

Preparation row for bud stitch: ch 1, 1 sc in first dc, *skip 1 dc, 2 sc in next dc, rep from *, ending 2 sc in second ch of ch 2, turn—19½ (21½, 23½) patts.

Patt row (bud stitch): ch 1, 1 sc in first sc, *skip 1 sc, 2 sc in next sc, rep from *, ending 2 sc in last sc. (Note that each pair of sc is worked in the second sc of pair as worked on previous row.) **
Rep patt row until back measures 8½ (9¾, 10½)", ending WS row.

BUD STITCH

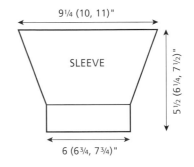
←pattern row

Button Border

First Side

Change to size 4.00 mm hook.

Row 1: ch 1, 1 sc in first sc, 1 sc in each of next 10 (12, 12) sc, sc2tog over next 2 sc, turn.

Row 2: ch 1, skip sc2tog, 1 sc in each of 11 (13, 13) sc, turn.

Row 3: ch 1, 1 sc in first sc, 1 sc in each sc to end. Fasten off.

Second Side

With RS of back facing and size 4.00 mm hook, leave 13 (13, 17) sts at center back, and rejoin yarn to next sc.

Row 1: ch 1, 1 sc in each of next 12 (14, 14) sc to end, turn.

Row 2: ch 1, 1 sc in first sc, 1 sc in each of 9 (11, 11) sc, sc2tog over last 2 sc, turn—11 (13, 13) sts.

Row 3: ch 1, 1 sc in first sc, 1 sc in each sc to end. Fasten off.

FRONT

Work as given for back to **.

Rep patt row until front measures 8 (8, 10) rows less than back at beg of button border, ending with a WS row.

Front Neck Shaping

First Side

Neck row 1: ch 1, 1 sc in first sc, [skip 1 sc, 2 sc in next sc] 7 (8, 8) times, turn—15 (17, 17) sts.

Neck row 2: ch 1, skip first sc, [skip 1 sc, 2 sc in next sc] 7 (8, 8) times, turn—14 (16, 16) sts.

Neck row 3: ch 1, 1 sc in first sc, [skip 1 sc, 2 sc in next sc] 6 (7, 7) times, turn—13 (15, 15) sts.

Neck row 4: ch 1, skip first sc, [skip 1 sc, 2 sc in next sc] 6 (7, 7) times, turn—12 (14, 14) sts.

Neck row 5: ch 1, 1 sc in first sc, [skip 1 sc, 2 sc in next sc] 5 (6, 6) times, turn—11 (13, 13) sts.

Work 3 (3, 5) more patt rows on these sts, ending length to match back at beg of button border and with a WS row.

Buttonhole Border

Change to size 4.00 mm hook.

Row 1: ch 1, 1 sc in first sc, 1 sc in each of next 10 (12, 12) sc, turn.

Row 2: ch 1, 1 sc in first sc, ch 2, skip 2 sc, 1 sc in each of next 3 (5, 5) sc, ch 2, skip 2 sc, 1 sc in each of 3 sc to end, turn.

Row 3: ch 1, 1 sc in each sc and 2 sc in each ch-2 sp to end. Fasten off.

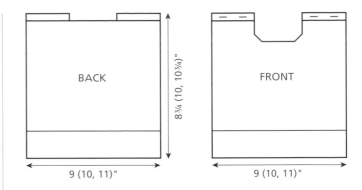

BACK

FRONT

8¾ (10, 10¾)"

9 (10, 11)"

9 (10, 11)"

9¼ (10, 11)"

SLEEVE

5½ (6¼, 7½)"

6 (6¾, 7¾)"

Second Side

With RS of front facing and size 4.50 mm hook, leave 9 (9, 13) sts at center front, and rejoin yarn to next sc.

Neck row 1: ch 1, skip sc at base of this ch, [skip 1 sc, 2 sc in next sc] 7 (8, 8) times to end, turn—14 (16, 16) sts.

Neck row 2: ch 1, 1 sc in first sc, [skip 1 sc, 2 sc in next sc] 6 (7, 7) times, turn—13 (15, 15) sts.

Neck row 3: ch 1, skip first sc, [skip 1 sc, 2 sc in next sc] 6 (7, 7) times to end, turn—12 (14, 14) sts.

Neck row 4: ch 1, 1 sc in first sc, [skip 1 sc, 2 sc in next sc] 5 (6, 6) times, turn—11 (13, 13) sts.

Work 4 (4, 6) more patt rows on these sts, ending length to match first side and with a WS row.

Buttonhole Border

Change to size 4.00 mm hook.

Row 1: work as for row 1 of first buttonhole border.

Row 2: ch 1, 1 sc in first sc, 1 sc in each of next 2 sc, ch 2, skip 2 sc, 1 sc in each of 3 (5, 5) sc, ch 2, skip 2 sc, 1 sc in last sc, turn.

Row 3: work as for row 3 of first buttonhole border. Fasten off.

SLEEVES (make 2)

With size 4.50 mm hook, ch 28 (32, 36).

Rosebud Border

Row 1 (WS row): 1 dc in third ch from hook, 1 dc in each ch to end, turn—27 (31, 35) sts.

Row 2: ch 2, skip first dc, 1 dc in each of next 2 (4, 2) dc, *skip 2 dc, dc3tog in next dc, inserting hook behind this dc3tog, work 1 dc in each of 2 missed dc, 1 dc in same place as dc3tog, 1 dc in each of next 2 dc, inserting hook into same place as base of dc3tog work dc3tog, 1 dc in each of next 3 dc, rep from *, ending 1 dc in each of 2 (4, 2) dc, 1 dc in second ch of ch 2, turn—3 (3, 4) pairs of leaves.

Row 3: ch 2, skip first dc, 1 dc in each of 2 (4, 2) dc, *skip top of dc3tog, 1 dc in next dc, ch 1, skip 1 dc, 1 popcorn in next dc, ch 1, skip 1 dc, 1 dc in next dc, skip top of dc3tog, 1 dc in each of next 3 dc, rep from *, ending 1 dc in each of 2 (4, 2) dc, 1 dc in second ch of ch 2, turn—3 (3, 4) motifs.

Row 4: ch 2, skip first dc, 1 dc in each of 3 (5, 3) dc, *1 dc in ch-1 sp, 1 dc in closing lp of popcorn, 1 dc in ch-1 sp, 1 dc in each of 5 dc, rep from *, ending 1 dc in each of 3 (5, 3) dc, 1 dc in second ch of ch 2, turn—27 (31, 35) sts. Rosebud border complete.

Inc row: ch 1, 1 sc in first dc, [1 sc in each of next 6 (7, 8) dc, 2 sc in next dc] 3 times, 1 sc in each of 4 (5, 6) dc, 1 sc in second ch of ch 2, turn—30 (34, 38) sc.

Patt row (bud stitch): ch 1, 1 sc in first sc, *skip 1 sc, 2 sc in next sc, rep from *, ending 2 sc in last sc, turn—31 (35, 39) sc.
Rep patt row 1 (3, 3) more times. 3 (5, 5) rows from last row of rosebud border, ending WS row.

Inc row 1: ch 1, 3 sc in first sc, *skip 1 sc, 2 sc in next sc, rep from *, ending 2 sc in last sc, turn.

Inc row 2: work as for inc row 1—35 (39, 43) sc.

Inc rows 3–6: work as for patt row.
Rep inc rows 1 and 2 once more—39 (43, 47) sc.
Rep patt row until sleeve measures 5½ (6¼, 7½)" or length required less ⅝". Fasten off.

FINISHING

Place buttonhole border over button border at each shoulder and stitch together at armhole edges. On back and front, count 20 (22, 24) rows down from base of each border and place a marker on side edge.
Join top edges of sleeves to armhole edges between markers. Join side and sleeve seams, matching patts.

Cuffs (make 2)

With RS facing and size 4.00 mm hook, join yarn to base of ch 1 at sleeve seam.

Picot Border

Round 1: ch 1, 1 sc in base of each ch, ending 1 sc under ch 1 at beg of round.

Round 2: ch 1, 1 sc in first sc, *ch 2, 1 sl st back in last sc worked, 1 sc in each of next 2 sc, rep from *, ending 1 sl st in first sc of round. Fasten off.

Lower Border

With RS facing and size 4.00 mm hook, join yarn to base of ch 1 at one side seam.
Work 2 rounds of picot border as for cuff.

Back Neck Border

With RS facing and size 4.00 mm hook, join yarn to corner of first side button border.

Row 1: ch 1, work 20 (22, 24) sc evenly spaced along back neck edge, turn.

Row 2: ch 1, 1 sc in first sc, 1 sc in each sc, working sc2tog at each inner corner, turn—18 (20, 22) sc.

Row 3: ch 1, 1 sc in first sc, *ch 2, 1 sl st back in last sc worked, 1 sc in each of next 2 sc, rep from * to end—9 (10, 11) picots. Fasten off.

Front Neck Border

With RS facing and size 4.00 mm hook, join yarn to corner of first side buttonhole border.

Row 1: ch 1, work 30 (34, 38) sc evenly spaced along neck edge, turn.

Row 2: ch 1, 1 sc in first sc, 1 sc in each sc, working sc2tog 4 times evenly spaced, turn—26 (30, 34) sc.

Row 3: work as for row 3 of back neck border—13 (15, 17) picots. Fasten off.
Sew on buttons to match buttonholes.
Press as instructed on yarn labels.

SLEEPING BAG

GENEROUSLY SIZED TO WEAR OVER NORMAL CLOTHES
(AND ALLOW FOR KICKING LEGS), THIS COZY SLEEPING BAG
IS IDEAL FOR TRAVELING.

SIZES

APPROXIMATE AGES	2–6 mos	6 mos–2 yrs
to fit height	25¾–28"	29½–32"
to fit chest	16"–18"	20"–22"
actual measurement	25½"	29½"
length to shoulder	21"	25"
sleeve seam with cuff folded back	6"	7"

MATERIALS

6 (7) balls of Fairytale DK by Patons (100% acrylic,
50g/178yds), col A (6344 Lapis) or comparable yarn
1 (1) ball of Fairytale DK by Patons, col B (6300 Snow
White) or comparable yarn
3.50 mm and 4.00 mm hooks
12 (14) buttons

GAUGE

16 dc and 8¾ rows = 4" in rows of dc with size 4.00 mm
hook

DOUBLE CROCHET ROWS

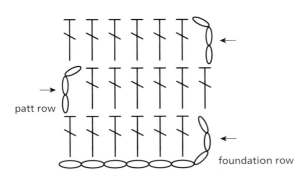

patt row

foundation row

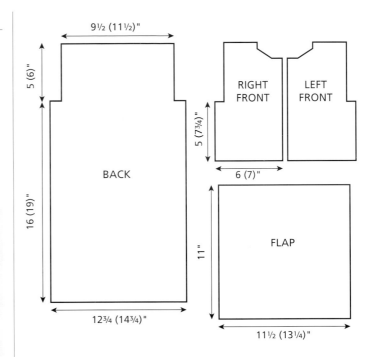

9½ (11½)"

5 (6)"

16 (19)"

BACK

12¾ (14¾)"

RIGHT FRONT

LEFT FRONT

5 (7¾)"

6 (7)"

11"

FLAP

11½ (13¼)"

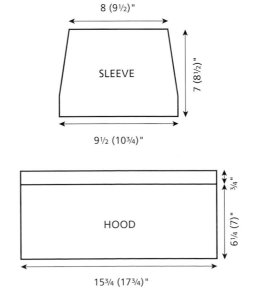

8 (9½)"

SLEEVE

7 (8½)"

9½ (10¾)"

¾"

HOOD

6¼ (7)"

15¾ (17¾)"

INSTRUCTIONS

BACK

With size 4.00 mm hook and col A, ch 54 (62).

Foundation row (RS row): 1 dc in fourth ch from hook, 1 dc in each ch to end, turn—52 (60) sts. (First ch 3 counts as first st.)

Patt row: ch 3, skip first dc, 1 dc in each dc, ending 1 dc in third ch of ch 3 at beg previous row, turn.

Rep patt row 34 (40) more times, ending WS row—36 (42) rows in all. Fasten off.

Armhole Shaping

With RS facing, skip first 7 dc, rejoin yarn to next dc.

Next row: ch 3, 1 dc in first dc, 1 dc in each of next 36 (44) dc, turn—38 (46) sts.

Rep patt row 10 (12) times, ending RS row—47 (55) rows in all. Fasten off.

FLAP

With RS of back facing, size 4.00 mm hook, and col A, join yarn to lower edge: skip base of first 3 dc, join yarn to base of next dc.

Row 1: ch 3, 1 dc in base of each of next 45 (53) dc, turn—46 (54) sts.

Rep patt row as for back 5 times.

Moon Motif

Use intarsia method (as page 13).

Row 1: with col A, ch 3, skip first dc, 1 dc in each of next 6 (9) dc, work 26 dc from row 1 of chart (reading right to left) in cols as shown, with col A work 1 dc in each of next 12 (17) dc, 1 dc in third ch of ch 3, turn.

Row 2: with col A, ch 3, skip first dc, 1 dc in each of next 12 (17) dc, work 26 dc from row 2 of chart (reading left to right) in cols as shown, with col A work 1 dc in each of next 6 (9) dc, 1 dc in third ch of ch 3, turn.

Cont in this way, reading from successive chart rows, until chart row 14 is complete—20 rows in all.

Cont in col A: rep patt row 4 more times—24 rows in all. Fasten off.

MOON MOTIF

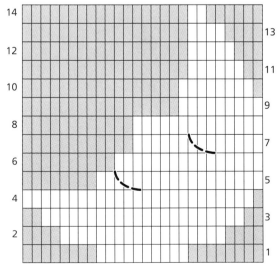

col A

col B

chain stitch using col A

LEFT FRONT

With size 4.00 mm hook and col A, ch 27 (31).

Work foundation row and row 1 as for back—25 (29) sts. Count foundation row as a WS row:

Rep patt row 9 (15) times, ending with a WS row—11 (17) rows in all. **

Fasten off.

Armhole Shaping

With RS facing, skip first 7 dc, rejoin yarn to next dc.

Next row: ch 3, 1 dc in next dc, 1 dc in each dc, ending 1 dc in third ch of ch 3, turn—18 (22) sts.

Rep patt row 5 (7) times, ending WS row.

Neck Shaping

Row 1: ch 3, skip first dc, 1 dc in each of next 13 (15) dc, dc2tog over next 2 dc, turn.

Row 2: ch 2, skip dc2tog, 1 dc in each dc, ending 1 dc in third ch of ch 3, turn.

Row 3: ch 3, skip first dc, 1 dc in each of next 11 (13) dc, dc2tog over last 2 dc, turn.

Row 4: work as for row 2—12 (14) sts.

Rep patt row once more. Fasten off.

RIGHT FRONT

Work as for left front to **.

Armhole Shaping

Next row: ch 3, 1 dc in first dc, 1 dc in each of next 16 (20) dc, turn—18 (22) sts.

Rep patt row 5 (7) times, ending WS row. Fasten off.

Neck Shaping

With RS facing, skip first 2 (4) dc, rejoin yarn to next dc.

Row 1: ch 2, 1 dc in each of next 14 (16) dc, 1 dc in third ch of ch 3, turn.

Row 2: ch 3, skip first dc, 1 dc in each of next 12 (14) dc, dc2tog over last 2 dc, turn.

Row 3: ch 2, skip dc2tog, 1 dc in each dc, ending 1 dc in third ch of ch 3, turn.

Row 4: ch 3, skip first dc, 1 dc in each of next 10 (12) dc, dc2tog over last 2 dc, turn—12 (14) sts.

Rep patt row once more. Fasten off.

SLEEVES (make 2)

Join shoulder seams. Begin at shoulder edge:

With RS facing, size 4.00 mm hook, and col A, join yarn at inner corner of armhole, ch 3, work 38 (44) dc evenly spaced along armhole edge, turn.

Rep patt row 3 (5) times—4 (6) rows in all.

Sleeve Shaping

Dec row 1: ch 2, skip first dc, 1 dc in each dc, ending 1 dc in third ch of ch 3, turn.

Dec row 2: ch 2, skip first dc, 1 dc in each dc to last dc, skip top of ch 2, turn.

Dec row 3: ch 3, skip first dc, 1 dc in each dc to last dc, skip top of ch 2, turn.

Dec row 4: ch 3, skip first dc, 1 dc in each dc, ending 1 dc in third ch of ch 3, turn—36 (42) sts.

Rep these 4 rows, twice more—32 (38) sts; 16 (18) rows in all.

Second Size Only

Rep patt row once more.

Both Sizes

16 (19) rows in all. Fasten off.

CUFFS (make 2)

Join sleeve seams, with first 4 rows worked matching armhole shapings.

With size 3.50 mm hook and col A, join yarn at base of sleeve seam.
Round 1: ch 1, 1 sc in first dc, 1 sc in each dc, ending 1 sl st in first sc of round.
Round 2: 1 sc in each sc of round, working [sc2tog over 2 sc] 4 times, evenly spaced.
Round 3: 1 sc in each sc.
Rep round 3 a total of 5 more times, ending at sleeve seam with 1 sl st in first sc of last round. 8 rounds in all. Fasten off.

HOOD

With size 4.00 mm hook and col A, ch 66 (74).
Work foundation row and patt row as for back—64 (72) sts.
Rep patt row 12 (14) times—14 (16) rows in all.
Border
Change to size 3.50 mm hook.
Dec row: ch 1, 1 sc in first dc, 1 sc in each of next 2 (3) dc, [sc2tog over next 2 dc, 1 sc in each of next 6 (7) dc] 7 times, sc2tog over next 2 dc, 1 sc in each of last 2 dc, 1 sc in third ch of ch 3, turn—56 (64) sts.
Next row: ch 1, 1 sc in first sc, 1 sc in each sc to end, turn.
Rep this row twice more. Fasten off.
Fold lower edge of hood in half and join to form center back seam. Sew side edges to neck edge, gathering evenly along front neck edges.

FRONT BANDS

Join side seams, matching row ends beneath armholes.
To Button Left Front over Right:
Right Front Band
With RS facing and size 3.50 mm hook, join col A at lower corner of back.
Row 1: ch 1, 2 sc in side edge of each row to corner, sc3tog at corner, 1 sc in base of each dc along lower edge of right front, 3 sc in same place at corner, 2 sc in side edge of each row up to beg of neck shaping, turn.
Row 2: ch 1, 1 sc in first sc, 1 sc in each sc, working 3 sc in second of 3 sc at outer corner and sc3tog at inner corner, to end, turn.
Rows 3 and 4: work as for row 2. Fasten off.
To Button Left Front over Right:
Left Front Band
Mark positions for 4 buttons on right front edge as follows: 1 at top, 2 sts down from neck edge; 1 at corner of right front; and 2 more evenly spaced between.
With RS facing and size 3.50 mm hook, join col A at top of left front edge.
Row 1: ch 1, 2 sc in side edge of each row to corner, 3 sc in same place at corner, 1 sc in base of each dc along lower edge of left front, sc3tog at corner, 2 sc in side edge of each row down to lower corner of back, turn.

Row 2: ch 1, 1 sc in first sc, 1 sc in each sc, working 3 sc in second of 3 sc at outer corner and sc3tog at inner corner, to end, turn.
Mark positions for 4 buttonholes to match positions for buttons on right front edge.
Row 3: work as for row 2, making a buttonhole to match each marker as follows: [ch 2, skip 2 sc].
Row 4: work as for row 2, working 2 sc in each ch-2 sp. Fasten off.
(To Button Right Front over Left:
Work left front band as above, omitting buttonholes, and mark positions for 4 buttons as given. Work right front band as above, making buttonholes to match markers as given.)
At each lower corner of back, fold band in toward center front and sew side edge of band to base of 3 dc at each side of flap.

FLAP BORDER

With RS facing and size 3.50 mm hook, join col A at lower right corner of flap.
Row 1: ch 1, 2 sc in side edge of each row to corner, 3 sc in same place at corner, 1 sc in each dc across top of flap, 3 sc in same place at corner, 2 sc in side edge of each row to lower left corner, turn.
Row 2: ch 1, 1 sc in first sc, 1 sc in each sc and 3 sc in second of 3 sc at each corner, to end, turn.
Mark positions for 9 (11) buttonholes as follows: 1 at center top to match lowest button on front edge; 1 at each corner of flap; 2 more on top edge, evenly spaced; 2 (3) on each side of flap, evenly spaced.
Row 3: work as for row 2, making a buttonhole to match each marker as follows: [ch 2, skip 2 sc].
Row 4: work as for row 2, working 2 sc in each ch-2 sp. Fasten off.
At each lower corner, sew down side edge of border.
Sew on buttons to match buttonholes.

STAR (make 3)

With size 3.50 mm hook and col B, ch 5 ch and join into a ring with 1 sl st in first ch made.
Round 1: *ch 3, 1 sc in second ch from hook, 1 hdc in next ch, 1 sl st in next ch of ring, rep from * 4 more times, ending with last sl st in base of first point of star. Fasten off.
Arrange the stars on the flap foll the photograph as a guide and stitch in place.
With col A, embroider mouth and eye on moon in chain stitch as indicated on chart.
Press as instructed on yarn labels.

LACY CARDIGAN

THIS CARDIGAN IS COOL AND PRETTY IN SMOOTH COTTON YARN.

SIZES

APPROXIMATE AGES	6–12 mos	1–2 yrs	3–4 yrs
to fit chest	20"	22"	24"
actual measurement	23¼"	24¾"	26½"
length to shoulder	10½"	12½"	14½"
sleeve seam	8"	9¾"	11½"

MATERIALS

6 (7, 9) balls of Twilley's Lyscordet (3-ply cotton, 25g), col A
(21 Ecru) *or* comparable yarn
2.50 mm and 2.00 mm hooks
4 (5, 6) small buttons

GAUGE

9½ patts and 17 rows = 4" in lacy pattern with size 2.50
mm hook

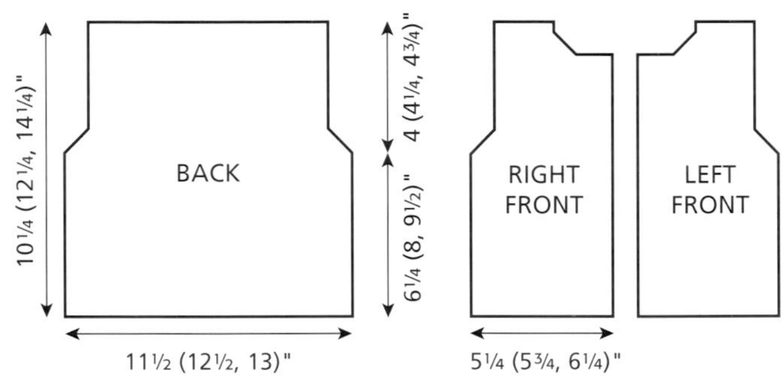

INSTRUCTIONS

BACK
With size 2.50 mm hook, ch 86 (92, 98).
Foundation row: 1 hdc in third ch from hook, *ch 1, 1 hdc in next
ch, skip 1 ch, 1 hdc in next ch, rep from *, ending 1 hdc in last ch,
turn—28 (30, 32) patts.
Patt row (lacy pattern): ch 2, *skip 2 hdc, [1 hdc, ch 1, 1 hdc] in
next ch sp, rep from *, ending skip last hdc, 1 hdc in second ch of
ch 2, turn.
Rep patt row until back measures 6¼ (8, 9½)", ending WS row.

LACY PATTERN

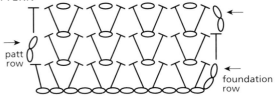

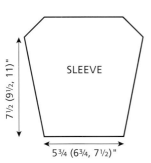

BACK	RIGHT FRONT	LEFT FRONT

10¼ (12¼, 14¼)"

4 (4¼, 4¾)"

6¼ (8, 9½)"

11½ (12½, 13)"

5¼ (5¾, 6¼)"

SLEEVE

7½ (9½, 11)"

5¾ (6¾, 7½)"

Armhole Shaping
Place a marker at each end of last row.
Dec row 1: ch 2, 1 hdc in first ch sp, work patt as set, ending
hdc2tog over last ch sp and second ch of ch 2, turn—26 (28, 30)
patts.
Dec row 2: ch 2 [1 hdc, ch 1, 1 hdc] in each ch sp, ending 1 hdc in
last hdc, turn.
Rep these 2 rows a total of 3 more times—20 (22, 24) patts.
Rep patt row until back measures 10¼ (12¼, 14)" in all, ending WS
row. Fasten off.

LEFT FRONT
With size 2.50 mm hook, ch 41 (44, 47).
Work foundation row and patt row as for back—13 (14, 15) patts.
Rep patt row until length matches back to beg armhole shaping,
ending WS row.
**Armhole Shaping
Place a marker at end of last row.
Dec row 1: ch 2, 1 hdc in first ch sp, work patt as set to end—12
(13, 14) patts.
Dec row 2: work patt as set, ending 1 hdc in last hdc, turn.
Rep these 2 rows a total of 3 more times—9 (10, 11) patts.
Rep patt row until length measures 8 (8, 10) rows less than back,
ending WS row.

FRONT NECK SHAPING
Row 1: ch 2, work 7 (7, 8) patts as set, 1 hdc in next ch sp, turn.
Row 2: work as for patt row.
Row 3: work patt as set to last ch sp, 1 hdc in last ch sp, turn.
Row 4: work as for patt row.
Rep rows 3 and 4 once more—5 (5, 6) patts.
Rep patt row 2 (2, 4) more times. Length matches back. Fasten off.

RIGHT FRONT
Work as for left front to **.
Armhole Shaping
Place a marker at beg of last row.
Dec row 1: work patt as set to last ch sp, hdc2tog over last ch sp and second ch of ch 2, turn—12 (13, 14) patts.
Dec row 2: ch 2 [1hdc, ch 1, 1hdc] in each ch sp, ending 1 hdc in second ch of ch 2, turn.
Rep these 2 rows a total of 3 more times—9 (10, 11) patts.
Rep patt row until length measures 8 (8, 10) rows less than back, ending WS row. Fasten off.
Front Neck Shaping
Rejoin yarn to second (third, third) ch sp of last row.
Row 1: ch 2, work 7 (7, 8) patts as set to end, turn.
Row 2: work as for patt row.
Row 3: 1 sl st in first ch sp, ch 2, work patt as set to end, turn.
Row 4: work as for patt row.

Rep rows 3 and 4 once more—5 (5, 6) patts.
Rep patt row a total of 2 (2, 4) more times. Length matches back. Fasten off.

SLEEVES (make 2)
With size 2.50 mm hook, ch 44 (50, 56).
Work foundation row and patt row as for back—14 (16, 18) patts.
Rep patt row 2 (4, 4) more times—4 (6, 6) rows.
Inc row 1: ch 3, 1 hdc in st at base of ch 3, work patt as set, ending [1 hdc, ch 1, 1 hdc] in second ch of ch 2, turn.
Inc row 2: ch 3, 1 hdc in first ch sp, work patt as set, ending [1 hdc, ch 1, 1 hdc] in ch-3 sp, turn.
Inc row 3 (3–4, 3–5): work as for inc row 2.
Inc row 4 (5, 6): ch 2, [1 hdc, ch 1, 1 hdc] in first ch sp, work patt as set, ending [1 hdc, ch 1, 1hdc] in last ch sp, 1 hdc in second ch of ch 3, turn—16 (18, 20) patts.
Inc rows 5–6 (6–8, 7–10): work as for patt row—10 (14, 16) rows in all.
Rep inc rows 1–6 (1–8, 1–10), twice more—20 (22, 24) patts; 22 (30, 36) rows.
Work inc rows 1–4 (1–5, 1–6) once again—22 (24, 26) patts.
Rep patt row until sleeve measures 7½ (9½, 11)" in all.
Top of Sleeve Shaping
Place a marker at each end of last row.
Dec row 1: ch 2, 1 hdc in first ch sp, work patt as set, ending hdc2tog over last ch sp and second ch of ch 2, turn—20 (22, 24) patts.

Dec row 2: work as for patt row.
Rep these 2 rows a total of 3 more times—14 (16, 18) patts. Fasten off.

FINISHING

Join shoulder seams. Join top edges of sleeves to armhole edges, matching shaping rows above markers. Join side and sleeve seams by slip stitching on WS, matching row ends.

Collar

With RS facing and size 2.00 mm hook, join yarn to neck edge at top of right front.

Row 1: work around neck edge: ch 1, 1 sc in each hdc and ch sp and 3 sc in side edge of each 2 rows, with sc3tog at each corner of back neck, along to top of left front edge, turn.

Row 2: ch 1, 1 sc in first sc, 1 sc in each st to end, turn.
Rep row 2 twice more.

Row 5: as row 2, working sc2tog, one or more times, evenly spaced to make 51 (57, 63) sts, turn.

Row 6: ch 2, skip first sc, *[1 hdc, ch 1, 1 hdc] in next sc, skip 1 sc, rep from *, ending [1 hdc, ch 1, 1 hdc] in next sc, 1 hdc in last sc, turn.

Row 7: ch 2, *skip 2 hdc, [1 hdc, ch 1, 1 hdc] in next ch sp, rep from *, ending skip last hdc, 1 hdc in second ch of ch 2, turn—25 (28, 31) patts.
Rep row 7, 4 (6, 8) more times. Fasten off.

Cuffs (make 2)

With RS facing and size 2.00 mm hook, join yarn to base of sleeve seam.

Shell Border

Round 1: ch 1, *1 sc in next ch sp, sc2tog over base of next 2 hdc, 1 sc in next ch sp, 1 sc in base of each of next 2 hdc, rep from *, ending 1 sl st in ch 1 at beg of round.

Round 2: ch 1, skip 1 sc, *[1 sc, 1 hdc, 1 sc] in next sc, 1 sl st in next sc, skip 1 sc, rep from *, ending 1 sl st in ch 1 at beg of round. Fasten off.

Note: It may be necessary to adjust sts on round 2 to make a complete number of shells: skip an extra sc before 1 sl st, one or more times, as required.

Front and Lower Edge Border

With RS facing and size 2.00 mm hook, join yarn at left front base of collar.

Row 1: ch 1, work 3 sc in side edge of every 4 rows down front edge, 3 sc in same place at corner, work along lower edge in same way as for first round of cuff, 3 sc at next corner, work up right front edge in same way as for left front edge to base of collar, turn.
Buttonhole band: ch 1, 1 sc in first sc, *ch 2, skip 2 sc, 1 sc in each of next 10 sc, rep from * 2 (3, 4) more times, ch 2, skip 2 sc, 1 sc in each sc to second of 3 sc at first corner, turn and work back: ch 1, 1 sc in each sc and 2 sc in each ch sp to end, turn. 4 (5, 6) buttonholes.

Row 2: ch 1, 1 sc in each sc to corner, 3 sc in same place, 1 sc in side edge of each row of buttonhole band, 1 sc in each sc along lower edge, 3 sc in second of 3 sc at corner, 1 sc in each sc to end, turn.
Button band: ch 1, 1 sc in each sc to second of 3 sc at first corner, turn and work back: ch 1, 1 sc in each sc to end, turn.
Shell row: ch 1, skip first sc, *[1 sc, 1 hdc, 1 sc] in next sc, 1 sl st in next sc, skip 1 sc, rep from *, ending 1 sl st in last sc at top of right front edge. Fasten off.

Note: it may be necessary to adjust sts in same way as for cuff to make the same number of shells on each front edge.

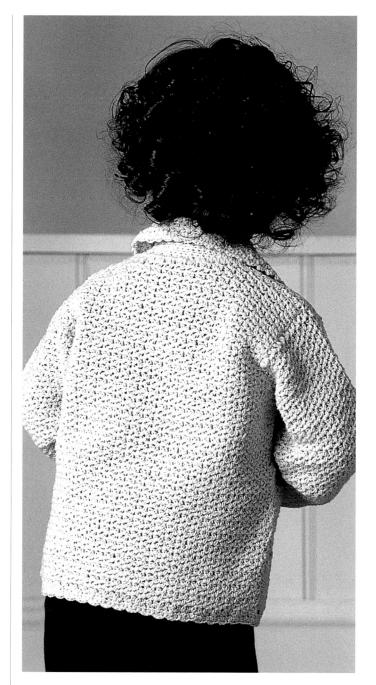

Collar Border

With underneath of collar facing and size 2.00 mm hook, join yarn at top corner of buttonhole band.

Row 1: ch 1, 3 sc across top of band, sc3tog at corner, 1 sc in side edge of each sc row, 3 sc in side edge of every 4 patt rows to corner, 3 sc in same place at corner, 1 sc in each hdc and ch sp across top of collar, 3 sc in same place at corner, work down second side of collar in same way as first side, sc3tog at corner, 3 sc across top of band, 1 sl st in first st of shell at corner, turn.

Shell row: (adjusting sts if necessary as before) ch 1, 1 sc in each sc to corner, sc2tog at corner, *skip 1 sc, [1 sc, 1 hdc, 1 sc] in next sc, 1 sl st in next sc, rep from *, ending at top of band, sc2tog at corner, 1 sc in each sc, 1 sl st in first st of shell on front edge.
Fasten off.

Sew on buttons to match buttonholes.

Press as instructed on yarn labels.

VEST WITH HOOD

THIS QUICK-TO-MAKE VEST IN DK YARN HAS A COZY HOOD AND
DRAWSTRING DETAILS.

SIZES

APPROXIMATE AGES	6–12 mos	1–2 yrs	3–4 yrs
to fit chest	20"	22"	24"
actual measurement	23½"	26"	28"
length to shoulder	12½"	14½"	16½"

MATERIALS

4 (5, 6) balls of Country Style DK by Sirdar (45% acrylic,
40% nylon, 15% wool, 50g/175yds), col A (477 Russet Red)
or comparable yarn
1 (1, 1) ball of Country Style DK by Sirdar, col B (411 Cream)
or comparable yarn
4.00 mm and 4.50 mm hooks
Open-ended zipper, 10 (12, 14)" long, col cream
Narrow cord, 63 (67, 71)" long, col red
4 cord toggles or suitable beads

GAUGE

7 patts and 12 rows = 4" in long and short stitch with size
4.50 mm hook

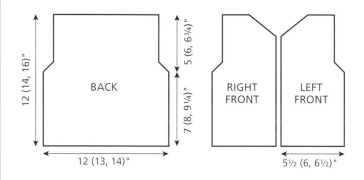

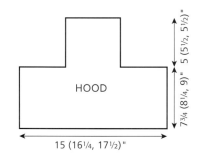

INSTRUCTIONS

BACK

With size 4.50 mm hook and col A, ch 44 (48, 52).
Foundation row (RS row): [1 dc, 1 hdc] in fourth ch from hook, *skip
1 ch, [1 dc, 1 hdc] in next ch, rep from * to end, turn—21 (23, 25)
patts.
Row 1 (long and short stitch): ch 2, *skip 1 patt, [1 dc, 1 hdc] in
sp before next patt, rep from *, ending [1 dc, 1 hdc] in ch-2 sp,
turn.
Rep this row until back measures 7 (8, 9¼)", ending with a WS row.

LONG AND SHORT STITCH

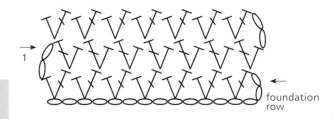

foundation
row

Armhole Shaping

Dec row 1: skip 1 hdc, 1 sl st in dc, ch 2, work patt as set to last
patt, skip 1 hdc, 1 hdc in next dc, turn—19 (21, 23) patts.
Dec row 2: ch 2, work patt as set to last patt, skip 1 hdc, 1 hdc in
next dc, turn—18 (20, 22) patts.
Rep dec row 2 a total of 5 more times—13 (15, 17) patts.
Work in patt as set until back measures 12 (14, 16)" in all. Fasten off.

LEFT FRONT

**With size 4.50 mm hook and col A, ch 22 (24, 26).
Work foundation row and row 1 as for back—10 (11, 12) patts.
Work in patt as set until front measures 7 (8, 9¼)", ending with a
WS row. **
Armhole Shaping

Dec row 1: skip 1 hdc, 1 sl st in dc, ch 2, work patt as set to end,
turn—9 (10, 11) patts.
Dec row 2: ch 2, work patt as set to last patt, skip 1 hdc, 1 hdc in
next dc, turn—8 (9, 10) patts.
Dec row 3: work patt as set, turn.
Rep dec rows 2 and 3 twice more—6 (7, 8) patts.

Work in patt as set until front measures 10 (12, 14)", ending at front edge with a RS row.

Neck Shaping

Row 1: ch 2, skip 1 patt, 1 hdc in sp before next patt, work patt as set to end, turn—5 (6, 7) whole patts.

Row 2: ch 2, work patt as set to last complete patt, 1 hdc in sp before patt, 1 hdc in second ch of ch 2, turn—4 (5, 6) patts.

Work row 1 (rows 1 and 2, rows 1 and 2) again—3 (3, 4) patts. Cont in patt as set until front measures 12 (14, 16)" in all. Fasten off.

RIGHT FRONT

Work as for left front from ** to **.

Armhole Shaping

Dec row 1: work patt as set to last patt, skip 1 hdc, 1 hdc in next dc, turn—9 (10, 11) patts.

Dec row 2: ch 2, work patt as set to end, turn.

Rep these 2 rows a total of 3 more times—6 (7, 8) patts.

Work in patt as set until front measures 10 (12, 14)", ending at armhole edge with a RS row.

Neck Shaping

Row 1: ch 2, work patt as set to last complete patt, 1 hdc in sp before hdc, 1 hdc in second ch of ch 2, turn—5 (6, 7) patts.
Row 2: ch 2, skip 1 patt, 1 hdc in sp before next patt, work patt as set to end, turn—4 (5, 6) patts.
Work row 1 (rows 1 and 2, rows 1 and 2) again—3 (3, 4) patts.
Cont until front measures 12 (14, 16)" in all. Fasten off.

HOOD

Join shoulder seams. With RS facing and size 4.50 mm hook, join col A at beg of neck shaping on Right Front.
Row 1: ch 2, [1 dc, 1hdc] in same place 9 (9, 10) times up right front neck shaping rows to shoulder seam, 7 (9, 9) patts as set across back neck edge, [1 dc, 1 hdc] in same place 9 (9, 10) times down left front neck shaping rows working last patt under ch 2 at beg of first neck shaping row, turn—25 (27, 29) patts.
Row 2: ch 2, work 8 (8, 9) patts as set, 2 patts in next sp, work 7 (9, 9) patts as set, 2 patts in next sp, work 8 (8, 9) patts as set to end—27 (29, 31) patts.
Work in patt as set until hood measures 7¾ (8¼, 8¾)" from neck edge. Fasten off.
Next row: with same side of work facing, rejoin yarn to sp foll ninth (tenth, tenth) patt, ch 2, work 9 (9, 11) patts as set, turn, leaving 9

(10, 10) patts unworked at end of row.
Cont in patt for 5 (5½, 5½)" more. Fasten off.
Join seams at top of hood. Join underarm seams.

ARMHOLE BORDERS (make 2)

With RS facing, and size 4.00 mm hook, join col B at top of underarm seam.
Round 1: ch 1, 3 sc in side edge of every 2 rows all around, ending 1 sl st in first sc of round.
Round 2: ch 1, 1 sc in each sc, ending 1 sl st in first sc of round. Fasten off.

FRONT, NECK, AND LOWER BORDER

Cut cord in half. Attach a toggle or bead to each cut end.
With RS facing and size 4.00 mm hook, join col B at lower corner of left front.
Round 1: ch 1, 1 sc in base of each ch along lower edge to corner 3 sc in same place at corner, 3 sc in side edge of every 2 rows up front edge, 1 sc in each st across top of hood, 3 sc in side edge of every 2 rows, ending 2 sc in same corner as first sc, 1 sl st in first sc of round.
Do not work too tightly:
Round 2: ch 1, *1 sc over first cord and into next sc, rep from *, ending in first sc of 3 at next corner, leave cord end at RS of work, 3 sc in next sc, 1 sc in each sc up right front edge to beg of neck shaping. Leaving second cord end at RS, work over second cord around edge of hood to beg of neck shaping on left front, leave cord end at RS, 1 sc in each sc down left front edge, ending 3 sc in last sc, 1 sl st in first sc of round. Fasten off.
Pin and tack zipper in place up front edges, with last round of crochet just clear of the zipper teeth. Use col B or matching thread to backstitch each sc in place. At neck edge, fold ends of zipper down underneath zipper edging as neatly as possible.
Press as instructed on yarn labels.

As an attractive variation, royal blue DK yarn (449) with matching blue cord for the drawstrings works well.

POLAR BEAR JACKET

A SIMPLE INTARSIA BEAR MOTIF AND ADD-ON
SNOWFLAKES DECORATE A SNUG JACKET TO KEEP OUT
WINTER CHILLS.

SIZES (see also page 58)

APPROXIMATE AGES to fit chest	1–2 yrs	3–4 yrs	5–6 yrs
	22"	24"	26"
actual measurement	23¾"	25½"	27½"
length to shoulder	13¼"	15¼"	17¼"
sleeve seam with cuff folded back	9¾"	11½"	13"

MATERIALS

4 (5, 6) balls of Country Style DK by Sirdar (45% acrylic,
40% nylon, 15% wool, 50g/175yds), col A (429 Lupin) or
comparable yarn
1 (1, 1) ball of Country Style DK by Sirdar, col B (412 White)
or comparable yarn
4.00 mm and 4.50 mm hooks
5 medium buttons

GAUGE

16 sts and 12 rows = 4" in rows of hdc with size 4.50 mm
hook.

Special Abbreviation: 1 rsc working from left to right (if
you are right handed): insert hook into next sc to right
with hook facing slightly downward, catch yarn and pull
through, turning hook back to normal position; yo, pull
through 2 lps on hook.

HALF DOUBLE CROCHET ROWS

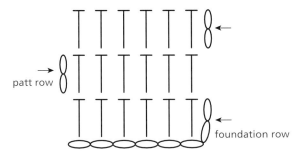

BACK

With size 4.50 mm hook and col A, ch 50 (54, 58).
Foundation row (RS row): 1 hdc in third ch from hook, 1 hdc in
each ch to end, turn—48 (52, 56) hdc.
Patt row: ch 2 (do not count as a st), 1 hdc in first hdc, 1 hdc in
each hdc to end, turn.
Rep patt row 6 (8, 12) more times—8 (10, 14) rows in all.
Polar Bear Motif
Use intarsia method (as page 13).
Row 1: with col A, ch 2, 1 hdc in first hdc, 1 hdc in each of next 6
(8, 10) hdc, work 33 hdc from row 1 of chart (reading right to left)
in cols as shown; with col A, work 1 hdc in each of 8 (10, 12) hdc to
end, turn.
Row 2: using col A, ch 2, 1 hdc in first hdc, 1 hdc in each of next 7
(9, 11) hdc, work 33 hdc from row 2 of chart (reading left to right)
in cols as shown; with col A, work 1 hdc in each of last 7 (9, 11)
hdc, turn.
Cont in this way, working successive chart rows until chart row
14 (16, 16) (WS row) is complete. Place a marker at each end of
last row.

POLAR BEAR MOTIF

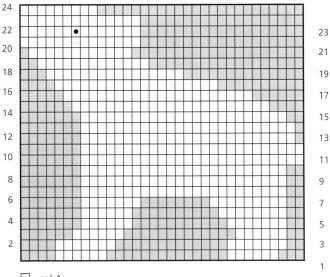

☐ col A
▨ col B
● French knot col A

56

Armhole Shaping

Cont reading from chart as set while shaping as follows:

Dec row 1: ch 1, skip first hdc, 1 hdc in each hdc to last hdc, skip last hdc, turn.

Rep this row 3 more times, ending chart row 18 (20, 20)—40 (44, 48) sts.

Work rem 6 (4, 4) chart rows in position as set.

Cont throughout in col A. Rep patt row 6 (10, 12) times—38 (44, 50) rows in all.

Fasten off.

LEFT FRONT

**With size 4.50 mm hook and col A, ch 25 (27, 29).

Work foundation row and patt row as for back—23 (25, 27) hdc.

Rep patt row 20 (24, 28) more times—22 (26, 30) rows in all.

**Place a marker at end of last row.

Armhole Shaping

Dec row 1: ch 1, skip first hdc, 1 hdc in each hdc to end, turn.

Dec row 2: ch 2, 1 hdc in first hdc, 1 hdc in each hdc to last hdc, skip last hdc, turn.

Rep these 2 rows once more—19 (21, 23) hdc.

Rep patt row 6 (8, 10) times—32 (38, 44) rows in all.

Front Neck Shaping

Row 1: ch 2, 1 hdc in first hdc, 1 hdc in each of next 14 (15, 16) hdc, turn.

Row 2: ch 1, skip first hdc, 1 hdc in each hdc to end, turn.

Row 3: ch 2, 1 hdc in first hdc, 1 hdc in each hdc to last hdc, skip last hdc, turn.

Row 4: work as for row 2—12 (13, 14) hdc.

Rep patt row twice—38 (44, 50) rows in all. Fasten off.

RIGHT FRONT

Work as for left front from ** to **. Place a marker at beg of last row.

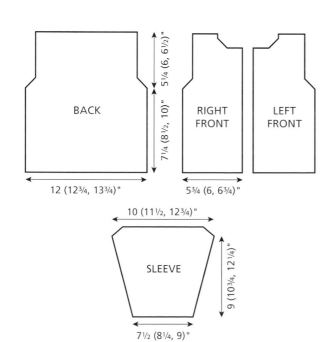

Armhole Shaping

Dec row 1: ch 2, 1 hdc in first hdc, 1 hdc in each hdc to last hdc, skip last hdc, turn.

Dec row 2: ch 1, skip first hdc, 1 hdc in each hdc to end, turn.

Rep these 2 rows once more—19 (21, 23) hdc.

Rep patt row 6 (8, 10) times—32 (38, 44) rows. Fasten off.

Neck Shaping

With RS of work facing, rejoin col A to fourth (fifth, sixth) hdc.

Row 1: ch 1, 1 hdc in next hdc, 1 hdc in each hdc to end, turn.

Row 2: ch 2, 1 hdc in first hdc, 1 hdc in each hdc to last hdc, skip last hdc, turn.

Row 3: ch 1, skip first hdc, 1 hdc in each hdc to end, turn.

Row 4: work as for row 2—12 (13, 14) hdc.

Rep patt row twice—38 (44, 50) rows in all. Fasten off.

SLEEVES (make 2)

With size 4.00 mm hook and col A, ch 32 (36, 38).

Work foundation row and patt row as for back—30 (34, 36) hdc.

Second and Third Sizes Only

Rep patt row twice more.

All Sizes

2 (4, 4) rows.

Sleeve Shaping

Inc row 1: ch 2, 1 hdc in first hdc, 1 hdc in each hdc to end, 1 hdc in second ch of ch 2 at beg of previous row, turn.

Inc row 2: work as for inc row 1.

Inc rows 3 and 4: work as for patt row—32 (36, 38) hdc; 6 (8, 8) rows.

Rep these 4 rows a total of 4 (5, 7) more times—40 (46, 52) hdc; 22 (28, 36) rows.

Rep patt row until sleeve measures 9 (10½, 12¼)" in all, ending WS row. Place a marker at each end of last row.

Top of Sleeve Shaping

Dec row 1: ch 1, skip first hdc, 1 hdc in each hdc to last hdc, skip last hdc, turn.

Rep this row a total of 3 more times—32 (38, 44) hdc. Fasten off.

FINISHING

Join shoulder seams. Join top edges of sleeves to armhole edges, matching markers and shaping rows. Join side and sleeve seams.

Front Bands and Lower Border

With RS facing and size 3.50 mm hook, join col A at corner of left front neck shaping.

Row 1: ch 1, 3 sc in side edge of every 2 rows down front edge to corner, 3 sc in same place at corner, 1 sc in base of each ch along lower edge to corner, 3 sc in same place at corner, 3 sc in side edge of every 2 rows up front edge, ending at beg of neck shaping, turn.

Row 2: ch 1, 1 sc in first sc, 1 sc in each sc and 3 sc in second of 3 sc at each corner, to end, turn.

To button left front over right: row 3: ch 1, 1 sc in first sc, [ch 2, skip 2 sc, 1 sc in each of next 7 (8, 9) sc] 4 times, ch 2, skip 2 sc, complete as row 2.

(To button right front over left: row 3: from top of right front count down 40 (44, 48) sc, place a marker on this st. Work as for row 2, ending in marked st, [ch 2, skip 2 sc, 1 sc in each of next 7 (8, 9) sc] 4 times, ch 2, skip 2 sc, 1 sc in last sc.)

Both versions: row 4: work as for row 2, working 2 sc in each ch-2 sp. Fasten off.
Sew on buttons to match buttonholes.

Collar
With RS facing and size 4.00 mm hook, join col A to center of top edge of right front band.

Row 1: ch 1, 2 sc in top edge of band, 11 (13, 14) sc along front neck edge, sc3tog at back neck corner, 1 sc in each hdc along back neck edge, sc3tog at corner, 11 (13, 14) sc along front neck edge and 2 sc along top edge of band to center of band, turn.

Row 2: ch 1, 1 sc in first sc, 1 sc in each sc to end, turn.

Row 3: ch 1, 1 sc in first sc, *[2 sc in next sc, 1 sc in each of next 2 sc] 4 times, 2 sc in next sc*, 1 sc in each sc to last 14 sc, rep * to * once more, 1 sc in last sc, turn—10 sts inc.

Row 4: work as for row 2. Rep this row a total of 8 (10, 12) more times, without turning work on last row.

Border row: 1 rsc in each sc to end. Fasten off.

Left Side Collar Border
With RS of collar facing and size 3.50 mm hook, join col A at top corner of left front band: ch 1, 1 sc in top edge of band, sc3tog at corner, 1 sc in side edge of each row of collar to corner. Fasten off.

Right Side Collar Border
Work as for left side collar border, beg at corner of collar and ending at corner of right front band.

Cuffs (make 2)
With RS facing and size 3.50 mm hook, join col A at base of sleeve seam.

Round 1: ch 1, 1 sc in base of each ch, ending 1 sl st in first sc of round—30 (34, 36) sc

Round 2: ch 1, 1 sc in first sc, 1 sc in each of next 4 (5, 6) sc, [sc2tog over next 2 sc, 1 sc in each of next 4 (5, 5) sc] 3 times, sc2tog over next 2 sc, 1 sc in each sc to end of round.

Round 3: 1 sc in each st of round.
Rep round 3 a total of 6 more times, ending 1 sl st in 1 sc at underarm (level with sleeve seam).

Border round: 1 rsc in each sc, ending 1 sl st in first rsc of round. Fasten off.

Snowflake (make 14)
With size 3.50 mm hook and col B, ch 4 and join into a ring with 1 sl st in first ch made.

Round 1: (work over starting end of yarn) ch 2, 1 dc into ring (first point made), *ch 2, 1 sl st through 2 front threads at top of point below, ch 2, dc2tog into ring, rep from * 4 more times (6 points made), ch 2, 1 sl st through 2 front threads at top of point below, ch 2, 1 sl st in top of first point. Fasten off, leaving a 10" end.
Pull gently on starting end to tighten center of snowflake. Secure and trim this end.

Arrange snowflakes on jacket, following photograph as a guide: 3 on back, 5 on front, and 3 on each sleeve. Use long end of yarn to stitch each snowflake in place.

Using col A, work a French knot for polar bear's eye as shown on chart.

Optional: with col B, work in chain stitch around outline of polar bear as shown in photograph.

Press as instructed on yarn labels.

OVERALLS

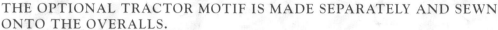

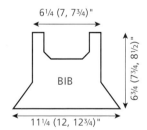

THE OPTIONAL TRACTOR MOTIF IS MADE SEPARATELY AND SEWN ONTO THE OVERALLS.

SIZES

APPROXIMATE AGES	6–12 mos	1–2 yrs	3–4 yrs
to fit chest	20"	22"	24"
to fit height	30"–32"	34"–36"	38"–40"
length to waist with cuff turned up	15¾"	17¾"	19½"
inside leg	10¼"	11¾"	13¼"

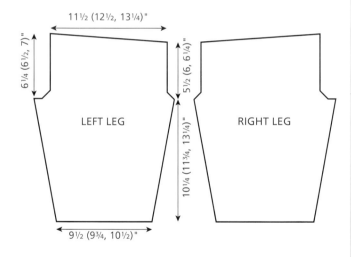

MATERIALS

4 (5, 6) balls of Calypso 4-ply by Sirdar (100% cotton, 50g/116yds), col A (654 Classic Denim) *or* comparable yarn
Optional: scraps of DK cotton yarn: col B (red) and col C (black)
3.00 mm and 3.50 mm hooks
2 medium buttons
⅝ yd. of ½"-wide elastic

GAUGE

19 sts and 23 rows = 4" in rows of sc with size 3.50 mm hook

Rep these 4 rows a total of 10 (11, 12) more times—68 (72, 76) sc; 48 (56, 62) rows.
Rep patt row until work measures 10 (11¾, 13½)", ending WS row.
*Place a marker at end of last row.

Crotch Shaping
Row 1: ch 1, sc2tog over first 2 sc, 1 sc in each sc to last 6 sc, sc2tog over next 2 sc, turn leaving last 4 sc unworked.
Row 2: ch 1, sc2tog over sc2tog and first sc, 1 sc in each sc to last 2 sts, sc2tog over last sc and sc2tog, turn.
Rep row 2 twice more—56 (60, 64) sts.
Rep patt row until work measures 15¾ (17¾, 19¾)", ending RS row.

Waist Shaping
Waist row 1: ch 1, 1 sc in first sc, 1 sc in each of next 36 (38, 40) sc, 1 sl st in next sc, turn.
Waist row 2: 1 sc in each sc to end, turn.
Waist row 3: ch 1, 1 sc in first sc, 1 sc in each of next 17 (18, 19) sc, 1 sl st in next sc, turn.
Waist row 4: work as for waist row 2.
Waist row 5: ch 1, 1 sc in first sc, 1 sc in each sc and sl st to end.
Fasten off.

LEFT LEG
Work as for right leg to *. Fasten off. Place a marker at beg of last row.

Crotch Shaping
With RS facing, rejoin yarn to fourth sc of last row.
Row 1: ch 1, sc2tog over next 2 sc, 1 sc in each sc to last 2 sc, sc2tog over last 2 sc, turn.
Row 2: ch 1, sc2tog over sc2tog and first sc, 1 sc in each sc to last 2 sts, sc2tog over last sc and sc2tog, turn.
Rep row 2 twice more—56 (60, 64) sts.

RIGHT LEG
With size 3.50 mm hook and col A, ch 47 (49, 51).
Foundation row (RS row): 1 sc in second ch from hook, 1 sc in each ch to end, turn—46 (48, 50) sc.
Patt row: ch 1, 1 sc in first sc, 1 sc in each sc to end, turn.
Rep patt row a total of 2 (6, 8) more times—4 (8, 10) rows in all.

Leg Shaping
Inc row 1: ch 1, 2 sc in first sc, 1 sc in each sc to end, turn.
Inc row 2: work as for inc row 1.
Inc rows 3 and 4: work as for patt row—48 (50, 52) sc; 8 (12, 14) rows.

Rep patt row until length matches right leg at beg of waist shaping, ending RS row.

Waist Shaping
Work 1 WS row. Work waist rows 1–4 as for right leg. Fasten off.

WAISTBAND
Join center front seam from waist edge down to markers. With RS facing and size 3.50 mm hook, join yarn to first sc at waist edge.
Row 1: ch 1, 1 sc in first sc, 1 sc in each sc and sl st to end, turn—112 (120, 128) sc.
Row 2: ch 1, 1 sc in back lp only (as work faces you) of each sc to end, turn.
Rows 3–6: work as for patt row. Fasten off.
With WS facing, rejoin yarn to empty front lp of first sc of row 2, ch

2, *1 dc in next front lp, ch 1, skip 1 front loop, rep from * to end, turn.
Next row: work through both thicknesses to form casing for elastic: ch 1, 1 sc in back lp of first sc of row 6 together with front lp of first dc behind, *1 sc in back lp of next sc together with front lp of ch behind, 1 sc in back lp of next sc together with front lp of dc behind, rep from *, working last sc together with second ch of ch 2 behind. Fasten off.

BIB
With RS facing and size 3.50 mm hook, rejoin col A to twenty-ninth (thirty-first, thirty-third) sc of last row of waistband.
Row 1: ch 1, 1 sc in next sc, 1 sc in each of next 52 (56, 60) sc, sc2tog over next 2 sc, turn—54 (58, 62) sts.
Row 2: ch 1, sc2tog over sc2tog and next sc, 1 sc in each sc to last 2 sts, sc2tog over last sc and sc2tog, turn—52 (56, 60) sts.
Rep row 2 a total of 8 more times—36 (40, 44) sts.
Next row: ch 1, 1 sc in sc2tog, 1 sc in each sc, ending 1 sc in sc2tog, turn.
Foll row: ch 1, sc2tog over first 2 sc, 1 sc in each sc to last 2 sc, sc2tog over last 2 sc, turn—34 (38, 42) sts.
Rep these 2 rows twice more—30 (34, 38) sts.
Rep patt row until bib measures 4 (4¾, 5¼)" from top of waistband, ending WS row.
Neck Shaping
First Side
Row 1: ch 1, 1 sc in first sc, 1 sc in each of next 9 sc, sc2tog over next 2 sc, turn.
Row 2: ch 1, sc2tog over sc2tog and next sc, 1 sc in each sc to end, turn.
Row 3: ch 1, 1 sc in first sc, 1 sc in each sc to last sc and sc2tog, sc2tog over last 2 sts, turn.
Row 4: work as for row 2—8 sts.
**Rep patt row until bib measures 6½ (7½, 8¼)" from top of waistband, ending WS row.
Next row: ch 1, sc2tog over first 2 sc, 1 sc in each of next 4 sc, sc2tog over last 2 sc. Fasten off.
Second Side
With RS of bib facing and size 3.50 mm hook, leave 5 (9, 13) sc at center front and rejoin col A to next sc.
Row 1: ch 1, sc2tog over next 2 sc, 1 sc in each of next 10 sc to end, turn.
Row 2: ch 1, 1 sc in first sc, 1 sc in each sc to last sc and sc2tog, sc2tog over last 2 sts, turn.
Row 3: ch 1, sc2tog over sc2tog and next sc, 1 sc in each sc to end, turn.
Row 4: work as for row 2. Complete as first side from ** to end.

FIRST STRAP

With RS facing and size 3.50 mm hook, rejoin col A to tenth (eleventh, twelfth) sc of last row of waistband.

***Row 1:** ch 1, 1 sc in each of next 8 sc, turn.

Rep patt row until strap measures 7¾ (8½, 9½)", or length required. (Note: straps are worn crossed at center back.)

Buttonhole row: ch 1, 1 sc in each of first 3 sc, ch 2, skip 2 sc, 1 sc in each of 3 sc to end, turn.

Next row: work as for patt row, working 2 sc in ch-2 sp.

Rep patt row once more.

Next row: ch 1, sc2tog over first 2 sc, 1 sc in each of next 4 sc, sc2tog over last 2 sc. Fasten off.

SECOND STRAP

With RS facing and size 3.50 mm hook, rejoin col A to tenth (eleventh, twelfth) sc after bib along last row of waistband.

Complete as first strap from *** to end.

FINISHING

Join center back seam and inside leg seams.

Bib and Strap Border

With RS facing, and size 3.00 mm hook, join col A at top of center back seam.

Round 1: ch 1, 1 sc in each sc along waistband to corner of strap, sc3tog at corner, 1 sc in side edge of each row to end of strap, [2 sc in sc2tog, 1 sc in each sc, 2 sc in sc2tog] across end of strap, 1 sc in side edge of each row to corner, sc3tog at corner, 1 sc in each sc to base of bib, 1 sc in side edge of each row to top of shoulder, work across top of shoulder in same way as top of strap, 1 sc in side edge of each row down neck shaping, sc2tog at corner, 1 sc in each sc across center front, sc2tog at corner, then complete the second half of edging in same way as first half, ending 1 sl st in first sc of round at center back. Fasten off.

Ankle Cuffs (make 2)

With RS facing and size 3.00 mm hook, join col A at base of inside leg seam.

Round 1: ch 1, 1 sc in base of each ch, ending 1 sc in first sc of round.

Round 2: 1 sc in each sc all round.

Rep round 2 a total of 4 more times, ending 1 sl st in 1 sc at inside leg. Fasten off.

Tractor Motif

Special Abbreviation: 1 dtr 1 double treble worked as follows: yo 3 times, insert hook as directed, yo, pull through work only, [yo, pull through 2 lps] 4 times.

Body (follow chart above right)

With size 3.50 mm hook and col B, ch 9.

Row 1: 1 sc in second ch from hook, 1 sc in each ch to end, turn—8 sc.

Row 2: ch 2, 1 sc in each sc to end, turn.

Row 3: ch 2, 1 sc in each sc, ending 2 sc under ch 2, turn—10 sc.

Row 4: ch 3, 1 sc in second ch from hook, 1 sc in next ch, 1 sc in each sc, ending 2 sc under ch 2, turn—14 sc.

Row 5: ch 4, 1 sc in third ch from hook, 1 sc in next ch, 1 sc in each sc to end, turn—16 sc.

Row 6: ch 1, 1 sc in each sc, ending 1 sc under ch 2, turn—17 sc.

Row 7: 6 ch, skip first 3 sc, 1 dtr in next sc, ch 3, skip 4 sc, 1 dtr in next sc, turn.

Row 8: ch 2, 1 sc in dtr, 1 sc in each of 3 ch, 1 sc in dtr, 1 sc in each of next 2 ch, 2 sc in next ch. Fasten off, leaving a long end.

TRACTOR BODY

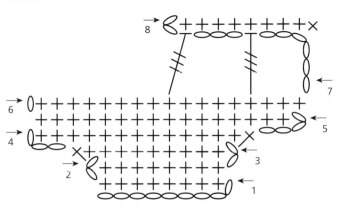

SMALL WHEEL   LARGE WHEEL

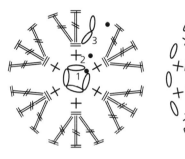 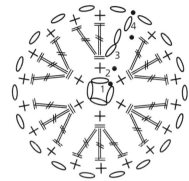

 = 3 double crochet in back loop

Large Wheel (follow chart above)

With size 3.50 mm hook and col B, ch 4 and join into a ring with 1 sl st in first ch made.

Round 1: (work over starting end) 6 sc into ring, 1 sl st in first sc of round. Fasten off.

Join col C to back lp only of first sc.

Round 2: (work over both yarn ends) ch 2, 2 dc in back lp of same sc, 3 dc in back lp of each of next 5 sc, 1 sl st in second ch of ch 2 at beg of round.

Round 3: ch 2, *1 sc in next dc, ch 1, rep from *, ending 1 sl st in first ch of ch 2. Fasten off, leaving a long end.

Small Wheel (follow chart above)

Work as for large wheel to end of round 2. Fasten off, leaving a long end.

Use the long ends to sew body and wheels to bib, following the photograph as a guide and backstitching around the edge of each piece.

Sew buttons to front shoulders, matching buttonholes on straps. With straps crossed at center back and buttoned to front, backstitch around the crossover in a diamond shape. Thread elastic through casing at waist, overlap the ends by 1", and backstitch securely.

Ankle cuffs may be worn folded up or down.

Press as instructed on yarn labels.

FLOWER MOTIF TOP AND BAG

COOL AND PRETTY, THIS TOP HAS A MATCHING BAG.

SIZES

APPROXIMATE AGES	6–12 mos	1–2 yrs	3–4 yrs
TOP			
to fit chest	20"	22"	24"
actual measurement	22½"	24¾"	27"
length to shoulder	12½"	14¾"	16¼"
sleeve seam	1¾"	2¼"	2½"
BAG	5" square		

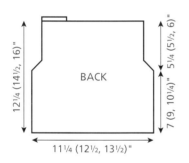

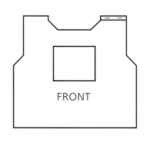

MATERIALS FOR THE SET

4 (4, 5) balls of Crystal DK by Patons (acrylic microfiber, 50g), col A (02673 Blossom) *or* comparable yarn
1 (1, 1) ball of Crystal DK by Patons, col B (02671 Cream) *or* comparable yarn
3.00 mm and 3.50 mm hooks
2 buttons for top
1 button for bag

GAUGE

20 sts and 10 rows = 4" in rows of dc with size 3.50 mm hook

MOTIF

↗ 1 sl st into edge of opening

TOP INSTRUCTIONS

BACK
With size 3.50 mm hook and col A, ch 59 (65, 71).
Foundation row (RS row): 1 dc in fourth ch from hook, 1 dc in each ch to end, turn—57 (63, 69) sts. (First ch 3 counts as first st.)
Dc row: ch 3, skip first dc, 1 dc in each dc, ending 1 dc in third ch of ch 3, turn. *
Rep this row a total of 16 (21, 24) more times—18 (23, 26) rows in all. Place a marker at each end of last row.

Armhole Shaping
Dec row 1: ch 2, skip first dc, dc2tog over next 2 dc, 1 dc in each dc to last dc and ch 3, dc2tog over last 2 sts, turn—55 (61, 67) sts.
Dec row 2: ch 2, skip dc2tog, dc2tog over next 2 sts, 1 dc in each dc to last dc2tog and ch 2, dc2tog over last 2 sts, turn—53 (59, 65) sts.
Rep dec row 2 twice more—49 (55, 61) sts.
Work 9 (10, 11) more dc rows, without shaping—31 (37, 41) rows in all, ending RS row.

Change to size 3.00 mm hook.
Button Border
Next row: ch 1, 1 sc in first dc, 1 sc in each of next 14 (16, 18) dc, turn.
Next row: ch 1, 1 sc in each sc to end, turn. Rep this row twice more. Fasten off.

FRONT

Work as given for back to *.

Rep dc row 11 (16, 19) more times. 13 (18, 21) rows in all, ending RS (WS, RS) row.

First Side: Opening for Motif

Next row: ch 3, skip first dc, 1 dc in each of next 17 (20, 23) dc, turn—18 (21, 24) sts.

Work 4 more rows on these sts only, ending at edge of opening—18 (23, 26) rows in all. Place a marker at side edge of last row.

Armhole Shaping

Dec row 1: ch 3, skip first dc, 1 dc in each dc to last dc and ch 3, dc2tog over last 2 sts, turn—17 (20, 23) sts.

Dec row 2: ch 2, skip dc2tog, dc2tog over next 2 sts, 1 dc in each dc, ending 1 dc in third ch of ch 3, turn—16 (19, 22) sts.

Dec row 3: ch 3, skip first dc, 1 dc in each dc to last dc2tog and ch 2, dc2tog over last 2 sts, turn—15 (18, 21) sts.

Dec row 4: work as for dec row 2—14 (17, 20) sts.

Work 1 more dc row—23 (28, 31) rows in all, ending RS (WS, RS) row. Fasten off.

Second Side: Opening for Motif

Leave 21 dc at center front and rejoin col A to next dc.

Next row: ch 3, 1 dc in each dc, ending 1 dc in third ch of ch 3, turn—18 (21, 24) sts.

Work 4 more rows on these sts—18 (23, 26) rows in all. Place a marker at side edge of last row.

Armhole Shaping

Dec row 1: ch 2, skip first dc, dc2tog over next 2 dc,1 dc in each dc, ending 1 dc in third ch of ch 3, turn—17 (20, 23) sts.

Dec row 2: ch 3, skip first dc, 1 dc in each dc to last dc2tog and ch 2, dc2tog over last 2 sts, turn—16 (19, 22) sts.

Dec row 3: ch 2, skip dc2tog, dc2tog over next 2 sts, 1 dc in each dc, ending 1 dc in third ch of ch 3, turn—15 (18, 21) sts.

Dec row 4: work as for dec row 2—14 (17, 20) sts.

Work 1 more dc row—23 (28, 31) rows in all, ending RS (WS, RS) row.

Work 21 ch. Fasten off with 1 sl st in top corner at opposite side of opening

Complete square opening: With WS (RS, WS) facing, rejoin col A to last dc of last row of first side.

Next row: ch 3, skip first dc, 1 dc in each of next 13 (16, 19) dc, 1 dc in each of next 21 ch, 1 dc in each of next 13 (16, 19) dc, 1 dc in third ch of ch 3, turn—49 (55, 61) sts.

Work 2 (3, 4) more dc rows—26 (32, 36) rows in all, ending WS row.

Neck Shaping

First Side

Row 1: ch 3, skip first dc, 1 dc in each of next 16 (18, 20) dc, dc2tog over next 2 dc, turn. 18 (20, 22) sts.

Row 2: ch 2, skip dc2tog, dc2tog over next 2 dc, 1 dc in each dc, ending 1 dc in third ch of ch 3, turn—17 (19, 21) sts.

Row 3: ch 3, skip first dc, 1 dc in each dc to last dc2tog and ch 2, dc2tog over last 2 sts, turn—16 (18, 20) sts.

Row 4: work as for row 2—15 (17, 19) sts; 30 (36, 40) rows in all, ending WS row.

Buttonhole Border

Change to size 3.00 mm hook.

Row 1: ch 1, 1 sc in first dc, 1 sc in each of next 14 (16, 18) sts, turn.

Row 2: ch 1, 1 sc in first sc, 1 sc in each sc to end, turn.

Row 3: ch 1, 1 sc in first sc, 1 sc in each of next 4 (5, 6) sc, ch 2, skip 2 sc, 1 sc in each of next 5 (6, 7) sc, ch 2, skip 2 sc, 1 sc in last sc, turn.

Row 4: ch 1, 1 sc in first sc, 2 sc in each ch-2 sp and 1 sc in each sc to end. Fasten off.

Second Side

With RS of front facing and size 3.50 mm hook, leave 11 (13, 15) dc at center front and rejoin col A to next dc.

Row 1: ch 2, dc2tog over next 2 dc, 1 dc in each dc, ending 1 dc in third ch of ch 3, turn—18 (20, 22) sts.

Row 2: ch 3, skip first dc, 1 dc in each dc to last dc2tog and ch 2, dc2tog over last 2 sts, turn—17 (19, 21) sts.

Row 3: ch 2, skip dc2tog, dc2tog over next 2 dc, 1 dc in each dc, ending 1 dc in third ch of ch 3, turn—16 (18, 20) sts.

Row 4: work as for row 2.

Work 1 dc row on these sts—31 (37, 41) rows in all, ending RS row. Fasten off.

Border of Square Opening

With RS of front facing and size 3.00 mm hook, join col A to first dc at lower right corner of opening.

Edging round: ch 1, 1 sc in each of next 19 dc, sc2tog at corner, 19 sc evenly spaced up side edge, ending sc2tog at next corner, 1 sc in base of each of next 19 ch, sc2tog at next corner, 19 sc evenly spaced down side edge, ending 1 sl st under ch 1 at beg of round. Fasten off.

Motif

Worked in rounds:

With size 3.50 mm hook and col B, ch 4 and join into a ring with 1 sl st in first ch made.

Round 1: (work over starting end of yarn) ch 1, 8 sc into ring, 1 sl st into first sc of round. Fasten off. Join col A to next sc.

Round 2: ch 4, tr2tog into sc at base of ch 4, *ch 4, tr3tog in next sc, rep from *, ending ch 4, 1 sl st in top of tr2tog. Fasten off. Rejoin col A to same place.

Round 3: ch 4, 1 sc in st at base of ch 4, *[4 sc in next ch-4 sp, 1 sc in top of next group] twice, ch 3, 1 sc in st at base of ch 3, rep from * twice more, 4 sc in next ch-4 sp, 1 sc in top of next group, 4 sc in next ch-4 sp, 1 sl st in first ch of ch 4 at beg of round.

Round 4: *[1 sc, ch 3, 1 sc] in corner lp, ch 5, skip 5 sc, 1 sc in next sc, ch 5, skip 5 sc, rep from *, ending 1 sl st in first sc of round.

Round 5: *[1 sc, ch 5, 1 sc] in corner lp, ch 5, skip 1 sc and 2 ch, 1 sc in next ch, ch 5, skip [2 ch, 1 sc, 2 ch], 1 sc in next ch, ch 5, skip 2 ch and 1 sc, rep from *, ending 1 sl st in first sc of round.

Change to size 3.00 mm hook. Join motif into opening with right sides of front and motif facing you:

Round 6: *3 sc in corner lp, 1 sl st in sc2tog at one corner of opening (inserting hook from back through to front), 3 sc in same corner lp, [3 sc in next ch-5 sp, skip 4 sc along edge of opening, 1 sl st through next sc, 3 sc in same ch-5 sp] 3 times, rep from *, ending 1 sl st in first sc of round. Fasten off.

Pull gently on starting end of yarn to tighten center of motif.

SLEEVES (make 2)

With size 3.50 mm hook and col A, ch 40 (44, 48).

Work foundation row and dc row as for back—38 (42, 46) sts. Rep dc row a total of 1 (2, 3) more times—3 (4, 5) rows.

Inc row: ch 3, 1 dc in first dc, 1 dc in each dc, ending 2 dc in third ch of ch 3, turn—40 (44, 48) dc. Place a marker at each end of last row.

Top of Sleeve Shaping

Dec row 1: ch 2, skip first dc, dc2tog over next 2 dc, 1 dc in each dc to last 2 dc and ch 3, dc2tog over last 2 dc, skip top of ch 3, turn—36 (40, 44) sts.

Dec row 2: ch 2, skip dc2tog, dc2tog over next 2 dc, 1 dc in each dc to last 2 dc, dc2tog over last 2 dc, skip dc2tog and top of ch 2, turn—32 (36, 40) sts.

Rep dec row 2 twice more—24 (28, 32) sts. Fasten off.

FINISHING

Join right shoulder seam.

Neck Border

With RS facing and size 3.00 mm hook, join col A to neck edge at corner of buttonhole border.

Row 1: work in sc all around neck edge, working 1 sc in side edge of each row of border, 2 sc in side edge of each row of dc, 1 sc in each dc and sc2tog at each inside corner, up to corner of button border, turn.

Row 2: ch 1, 1 sc in first sc, 1 sc in each sc to end, working sc2tog at each inside corner. Fasten off.

Place buttonhole border over button border and sew down at armhole edge.

Sew top edges of sleeves to armhole edges, stretching slightly to fit between markers.

Join sleeve seams. Join side seams, leaving lowest 5 rows unstitched at each side.

Sleeve Border (make 2)

With RS facing and size 3.00 mm hook, join col A to base of sleeve seam.

Round 1: ch 1, 1 sc in base of each ch all around, ending 1 sl st in first sc of round. Fasten off.

Lower Border

With RS facing, and size 3.00 mm hook, join col A to one corner of lower edge.

Round 1: ch 1, work all around in sc: 1 sc in base of each ch along lower edges, 3 sc in same place at each outer corner, 2 sc in side edge of each row of side splits, sc3tog at top of each side split, ending at first corner with 2 sc in same place as first st, 1 sl st in first sc of round. Fasten off. Sew on buttons to match buttonholes. Press as instructed on yarn labels.

BAG INSTRUCTIONS

FRONT AND BACK (make 2)

With size 3.50 mm hook, work rounds 1–3 of motif as for front of top.

Round 4: 1 sl st in ch-3 sp, ch 5, 1 dc in same ch-3 sp, *1 dc in each of next 11 sc, [1 dc, ch 3, 1 dc] in ch-3 sp, rep from * twice more, 1 dc in each of next 11 sc, 1 sl st in second ch of ch 5 at beg of round.

Round 5: 1 sl st in ch-3 sp, ch 5, 1 dc in same ch-3 sp, *1 dc in each of next 13 dc, [1 dc, ch 3, 1 dc] in ch-3 sp, rep from * twice more, 1 dc in each of next 13 dc, 1 sl st in second ch of ch 5 at beg of round.

Round 6: 1 sl st in ch-3 sp, ch 5, 1 dc in same ch-3 sp, *1 dc in each of next 15 dc, [1 dc, ch 3, 1 dc] in ch-3 sp, rep from * twice more, 1 dc in each of next 15 dc, 1 sl st in second ch of ch 5 at beg of round. Fasten off.

FINISHING

Place front and back with WS together. With size 3.00 mm hook, join col A to both ch-3 sps at one corner.

Edging round: ch 110 for strap (or length required), 2 sc in both ch-3 sps at next corner, work through both thicknesses: *1 sc in each of next 17 dc, [2 sc, ch 2, 2 sc] in ch-3 sp at next corner, rep from * once more, 1 sc in each of next 17 dc, 2 sc in ch-3 sp at base of strap, 1 sc in each of next 110 ch, 1 sl st in first sc at next corner. Fasten off.

Edge of Opening

With RS of back facing and size 3.00 mm hook, join col A to ninth of 17 dc along open edge, ch 7, 1 sl st in dc at base of ch 7, 1 sc in each of next 8 dc, 1 sc in ch-3 sp, 1 sl st in base of strap, turn and work along other edge of opening: 1 sc in ch-3 sp, 1 sc in each of 17 dc, 1 sc in ch-3 sp, 1 sl st in base of strap, turn and complete first edge: 1 sc in ch-3 sp, 1 sc in each of 8 dc, 1 sc in dc at base of ch lp, 10 sc into lp, 1 sl st in next sc. Fasten off.

Sew on button to match loop. Press as instructed on yarn labels.

JUMPER

THIS JUMPER IS FRESH AND PRETTY IN COOL COTTON AND CAN BE WORN BY ITSELF OR OVER A T-SHIRT.

SIZES

APPROXIMATE AGES	6–12 mos	1–2 yrs	3–4 yrs
to fit chest	20"	22"	24"
actual measurement at underarm	20"	22½"	24¾"
length to shoulder	17"	19"	21"

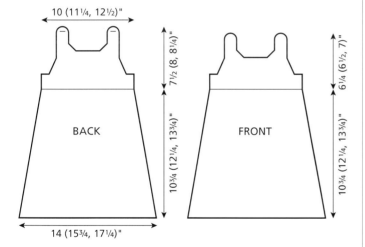

INSTRUCTIONS

BACK

Bodice
With size 3.00 mm hook and col A, ch 68 (76, 84).
Foundation row: skip 3 ch, *2 sc in next ch, skip 1 ch, rep from *, ending 2 sc in last ch, turn.
Patt row (bushy stitch): ch 2, *skip 1 sc, 2 sc in next sc, rep from * to end, turn—33 (37, 41) patts.

BUSHY STITCH

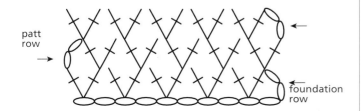

MATERIALS

9 (10, 11) balls of Twilleys Lyscordet (100% cotton, 25g), col A (78 White) *or* comparable yarn
1 (1, 1) ball of Twilleys Lyscordet, col B (87 Pale Pink) *or* comparable yarn
2.50 mm and 3.00 mm hooks
2 buttons

GAUGE

26 sts and 26 rows = 4" in bushy stitch with size 3.00 mm hook
7½ patts and 16 rows = 4" in star pattern with size 3.00 mm hook

Rep this row a total of 4 (6, 8) more times—6 (8, 10) rows in all.
Armhole Shaping
Dec row 1: sl st across first 4 sc, ch 1, [skip 1 sc, 2 sc in next sc] 28 (32, 36) times, skip 1 sc, 1 sc in next sc, turn, leaving last 4 sc unworked.
Dec row 2: ch 1, skip 2 sc, *2 sc in next sc, skip 1 sc, rep from *, ending skip last sc, 1 sc in ch 1, turn.
Dec row 3: ch 1, skip 2 sc, *2 sc in next sc, skip 1 sc, rep from *, ending 1 sc in last sc, turn.
Rep dec row 3 a total of 7 (9, 11) more times—19 (21, 23) patts.
Next row: ch 2, skip 2 sc, *2 sc in next sc, skip 1 sc, rep from *, ending 2 sc in last sc, turn. **
Rep bushy stitch patt row until work measures 2" from last shaping row, ending WS row.
Back Neck Shaping
First Side
Row 1: ch 2, [skip 1 sc, 2 sc in next sc] 6 times, skip 1 sc, 1 sc in next sc, turn.
Row 2: ch 1, skip 2 sc, work patt as set to end, turn.
Row 3: ch 2, *skip 1 sc, 2 sc in next sc, rep from * to last 2 sc, skip 1 sc, 1 sc in last sc, turn.
Row 4: work as for row 2.
Rows 5 and 6: work as for rows 3 and 2—4 patts.
***Work in patt until bodice measures 6¾ (7, 7½)" in all ending WS row.
Buttonhole row: ch 2, skip 1 sc, 3 sc in next sc, ch 2, skip 5 sc, 3 sc in last sc, turn.
Next row: ch 2, *skip 1 st, 2 sc in next st, rep from * to end, turn.
Last row: ch 1, skip 1 sc, 1 sc in next sc, [skip 1 sc, 2 sc in next sc] twice, skip 1 sc, 1 sl st in next sc. Fasten off.
Second Side
With RS facing, leave 11 (13, 15) sc at center front and rejoin col A

to next sc.

Row 1: ch 1, skip 1 sc, [2 sc in next sc, skip 1 sc] 5 times, 2 sc in last sc, turn.

Row 2: ch 2, [skip 1 sc, 2 sc in next sc] 5 times, skip 1 sc, 1 sc in next sc, turn.

Row 3: ch 1, skip 2 sc, 2 sc in next sc, work patt as set to end, turn.

Row 4: ch 2, [skip 1 sc, 2 sc in next sc] 4 times, skip 1 sc, 1 sc in next sc, turn.

Row 5: work as for row 3.

Row 6: ch 2, [skip 1 sc, 2 sc in next sc] 4 times, turn.

Work as for first side from *** to end.

Skirt

With RS facing and size 3.00 mm hook, join col A to base loop of first ch made.

Preparation row: work in base lps of foundation ch: ch 2, 2 dc in lp at base of these 2 ch, *skip 1 ch, [1 sc, 2 dc] in next ch, skip 2 ch, [1 sc, 2 dc] in next ch, rep from * to last 4 (2, 0) sts, then:

First Size Only

*Skip 1 ch, [1 sc, 2 dc] in next ch, rep from * once, 1 sc in base of ch 3 at beg row 1 of bodice, turn.

Second Size Only

Skip 1 ch, [1 sc, 2 dc] in next ch, 1 sc in base of ch 3 at beg row 1 of bodice, turn.

Third Size Only

1 sc in base of ch 3 at beg row 1 of bodice, turn.

All Sizes

27 (30, 33) patts.

Row 1 (Star Pattern): ch 2, 2 dc in sc at base of ch 2, *skip 2 dc, [1 sc, 2 dc] in next sc, rep from *, ending skip 2 dc, 1 sc in second ch of ch 2 at beg previous row, turn.

Rep this row until skirt measures 11½ (13, 14½)", or length required, ending WS row. Fasten off.

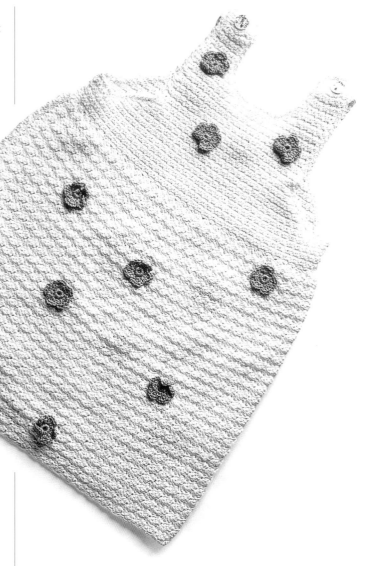

STAR PATTERN

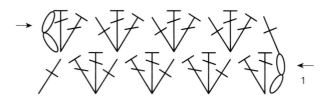

1

FRONT

Bodice

Work as given for back to **.

Work 1 patt row, ending WS row.

Front Neck Shaping

First Side

Work rows 1–6 as for first side of back neck shaping.

****Work in patt until bodice measures 6¼ (6¾, 7)" in all.

Last row: ch 1, skip 1 sc, 1 sc in next sc, [skip 1 sc, 2 sc in next sc] twice, skip 1 sc, 1 sl st in next sc. Fasten off.

Second Side

With RS facing, leave 11 (13, 15) sc at center front and rejoin col A to next sc.

Work rows 1–6 as for second side of back neck shaping.

Work as for first side from **** to end.

SKIRT

Work as for back.

FINISHING

Join side seams by slip stitching on wrong side, matching row ends.

Neck and Armhole Border

With RS facing and size 2.50 mm hook, join col A at left underarm seam, ch 1, then work all around top edge in sc, working 1 sc in each st and 1 sc in side edge of each row, with 3 sc in same place at top corners of each strap, ending 1 sl st under ch 1 at beg of round.

Edging round: *[1 sl st, ch 1, 1 sc] in next sc, skip 1 sc, rep from *, ending 1 sl st under first ch of round. (If necessary, end 1 sl st, ch 1, sc2tog over last 2 sc, 1 sl st under first ch of round.) Fasten off.

Sew a button to the front of each shoulder to correspond with the buttonholes.

Lower Border

With RS facing and size 2.50 mm hook, join col A to base of one side seam, ch 1, then work 1 sc in each dc and 1 sl st in each sc, all around lower edge, ending 1 sl st under ch 1 at beg of round. Fasten off.

Flower (make about 20)

With size 2.50 mm hook and col B, ch 5 and join into a ring with 1 sl st in first ch made.

Round 1: (work over starting end of yarn) ch 1, 10 sc into ring, 1 sl st under ch 1 at beg of round.

Round 2: *ch 2, 3 dc in next sc, ch 2, 1 sl st in next sc, rep from * 4 more times, ending with last sl st in sc at base of ch 2. Fasten off, leaving about a 10" tail.

Pull gently on starting end of yarn to tighten center of flower. Weave in end.

Arrange half the flowers on the front of the jumper and half on the back, following the photograph as a guide. Use the long end of yarn to stitch down each flower with tiny backstitches around the center circle.

Press as instructed on yarn labels.

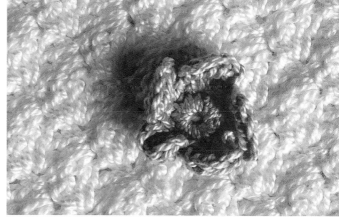

TARTAN CROPPED JACKET AND BERET

TRY THE TECHNIQUE OF WOVEN CROCHET: THE GARMENT PIECES
ARE WORKED WITH A PATTERN GRID OF MESH HOLES, THEN THE
CONTRASTING COLORS ARE WOVEN THROUGH THE MESH.

SIZES

APPROXIMATE AGES	6–12 mos	1–2 yrs	3–4 yrs
JACKET			
to fit chest	20"	22"	24"
actual measurement	23"	25"	28"
length to shoulder	10¼"	11½"	13¼"
sleeve seam with cuff folded back	8"	9¾"	11¼"
BERET			
to fit head	18"	19"	20"

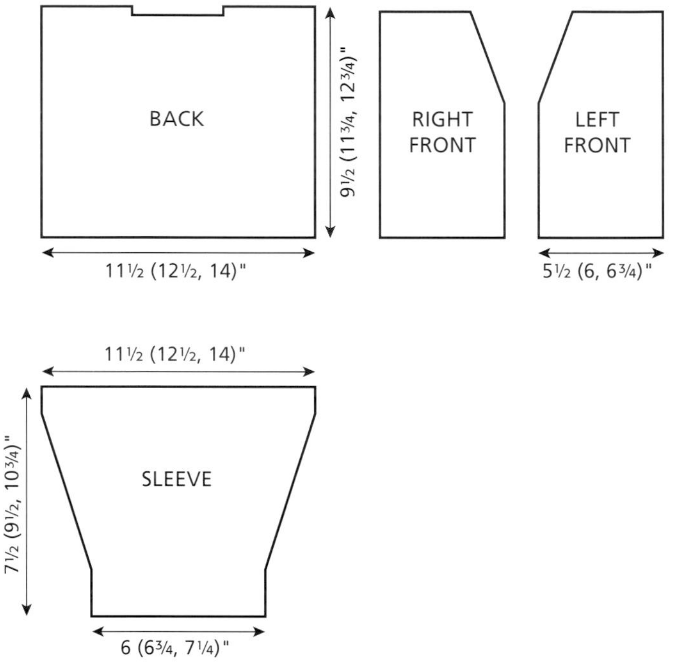

BACK — 9½ (11¾, 12¾)" — 11½ (12½, 14)"

RIGHT FRONT   LEFT FRONT — 5½ (6, 6¾)"

SLEEVE — 11½ (12½, 14)" — 7½ (9½, 10¾)" — 6 (6¾, 7¼)"

GRID PATTERN A

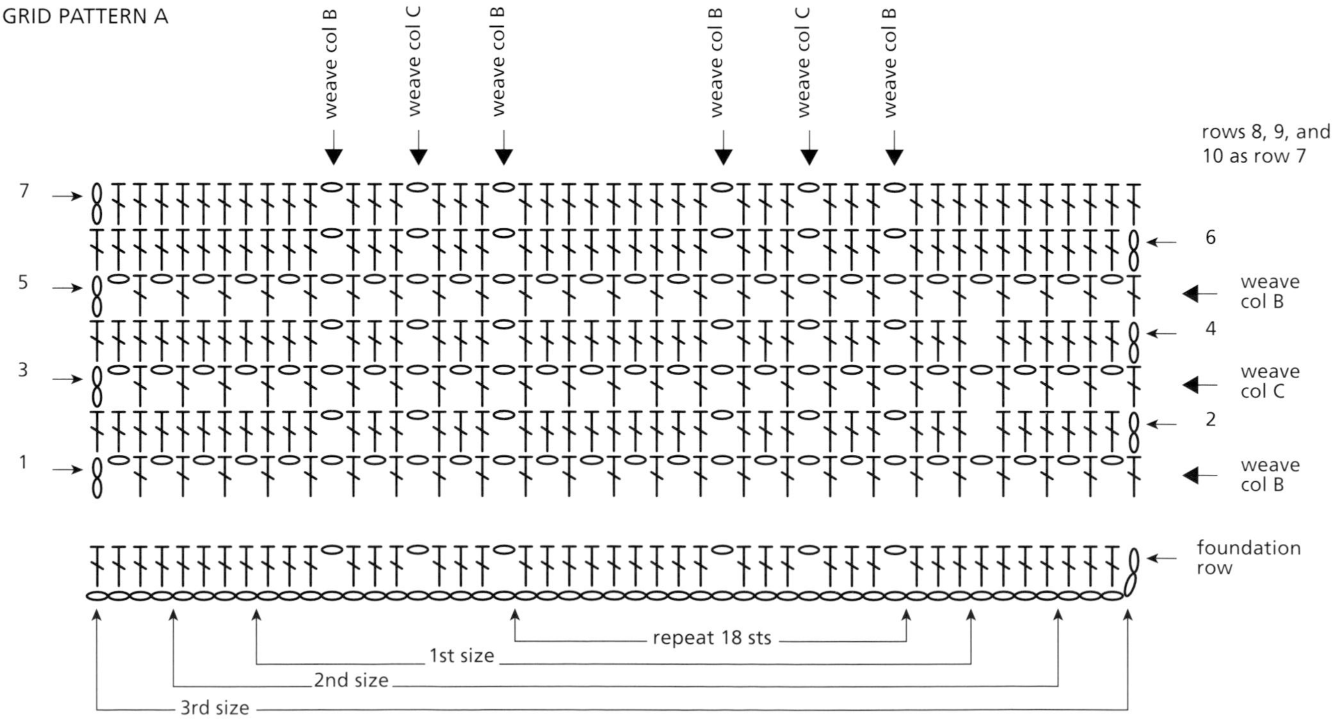

weave col B   weave col C   weave col B   weave col B   weave col C   weave col B

rows 8, 9, and 10 as row 7

7
6
5 — weave col B
4
3 — weave col C
2
1 — weave col B

foundation row

repeat 18 sts

1st size
2nd size
3rd size

MATERIALS FOR THE SET

3 (4, 4) balls of Jaeger Matchmaker Merino 4-ply (100% wool, 50g/200yds), col A (697 Peony) *or* comparable yarn
1 (1, 1) ball of Jaeger Matchmaker Merino 4-ply, col B (713 Meadow) *or* comparable yarn
1 (1, 1) ball of Jaeger Matchmaker Merino 4-ply, col C (740 Baltic Blue) *or* comparable yarn
2.50 mm and 3.00 mm hooks
Blunt-ended tapestry needle for weaving
4 buttons for jacket

GAUGE

Jacket: 24 sts and 12 rows = 4" in grid pattern with size 3.00 mm hook
Beret: First 8 rounds = 4" in diameter with size 3.00 mm hook

Special Abbreviation: 1 rsc working from left to right (if you are right-handed): insert hook into next sc to right with hook facing slightly downwards, catch yarn and pull through, turning hook back to normal position; yo, pull through 2 lps on hook.

JACKET INSTRUCTIONS

BACK
GRID PATTERN A
Row 1: ch 3, skip first 2 dc, *1 dc in next dc, ch 1, skip 1 st (which may be 1 dc or ch 1), rep from *, ending 1 dc in second ch of ch 2 at beg previous row, turn.
Row 2: ch 2, skip first dc, [1 dc in ch-1 sp, 1 dc in next dc] 1 (3, 5) times, *[ch 1, skip 1 ch, 1 dc in next dc, 1 dc in ch-1 sp, 1 dc in next dc] twice, ch 1, skip 1 ch, [1 dc in next dc, 1 dc in ch-1 sp] 4 times, 1 dc in next dc, rep from *, ending [1 dc in next dc, 1 dc in ch-1 sp] 1 (3, 5) times, 1 dc in second ch of ch 3, turn.
Rows 3–6: work as for rows 1 and 2, twice.
Row 7: ch 2, skip first dc, 1 dc in each of next 2 (6, 10) dc, *[ch 1, skip 1 ch, 1 dc in each of next 3 dc] twice, ch 1, skip 1 ch, 1 dc in each of next 9 dc, rep from *, ending 1 dc in each of next 2 (6, 10) dc, 1 dc in second ch of ch 2, turn.
Rows 8, 9, and 10: work as for row 7.
These 10 rows form grid pattern A. Repeat them as given below. With size 3.00 mm hook and col A, ch 70 (78, 86).
Foundation row (RS row): 1 dc in third ch from hook, 1 dc in each of next 1 (5, 9) ch, *[ch 1, skip 1 ch, 1 dc in each of next 3 ch] twice, ch 1, skip 1 ch, 1 dc in each of next 9 ch, rep from * twice more, work [ ] twice, ch 1, skip 1 ch, 1 dc in each of next 3 (7, 11) ch to end, turn—69 (77, 85) sts.
Beginning grid pattern A row 1 (7, 1), work 27 (31, 37) rows, ending grid pattern A row 7—28 (32, 38) rows in all.
Back Neck Shaping
First Side
Next row: ch 2, skip first dc, 1 dc in each of next 2 (6, 10) dc, [ch 1, skip 1 ch, 1 dc in each of next 3 dc] twice, ch 1, skip 1 ch, 1 dc in each of next 9 (7, 5) dc, dc2tog over next 2 sts. Fasten off.
Second Side
With RS of back facing, leave 23 (27, 31) sts at center, join col A to next st, ch 1, 1 dc in next st, work patt as set to end. Fasten off.

LEFT FRONT
GRID PATTERN B
Row 1: ch 3, skip first 2 dc, *1 dc in next dc, ch 1, skip 1 st (which may be 1 dc or ch 1), rep from *, ending 1 dc in second ch of ch 2 at beg previous row, turn.
Row 2: ch 2, skip first dc, [1 dc in ch-1 sp, 1 dc in next dc] 1 (3, 5) times, *[ch 1, skip 1 ch, 1 dc in next dc, 1 dc in ch-1 sp, 1 dc in next dc] twice, ch 1, skip 1 ch, [1 dc in next dc, 1 dc in ch-1 sp] 4 times, 1 dc in next dc, rep from *, ending 1 dc in last dc, 1 dc in ch-3 sp, 1 dc in second ch of ch 3, turn.
Rows 3–6: work as for rows 1 and 2, twice.
Row 7: ch 2, skip first dc, 1 dc in each of next 2 dc, *[ch 1, skip 1 ch, 1 dc in each of next 3 dc] twice, ch 1, skip 1 ch, 1 dc in each of next 9 dc, rep from *, ending 1 dc in each of next 2 (6, 10) dc, 1 dc in second ch of ch 2, turn.
Row 8: ch 2, skip first dc, 1 dc in each of next 2 (6, 10) dc, *[ch 1, skip 1 ch, 1 dc in each of next 3 dc] twice, ch 1, skip 1 ch, 1 dc in each of next 9 dc, rep from *, ending 1 dc in each of next 2 dc, 1 dc in second ch of ch 2, turn.
Rows 9 and 10: work as for rows 7 and 8.
These 10 rows form grid pattern B. Repeat them as given below. With size 3.00 mm hook and col A, ch 34 (38, 42).
Foundation row (RS row): 1 dc in third ch from hook, 1 dc in each of next 1 (5, 9) ch, *[ch 1, skip 1 ch, 1 dc in each of next 3 ch] twice, ch 1, skip 1 ch, 1 dc in each of next 9 ch, rep from *, ending 1 dc in each of next 3 ch to end, turn—33 (37, 41) sts.
Beginning grid pattern B row 1 (7, 1), work 15 (17, 21) rows, ending grid pattern B row 3 (WS row)—16 (18, 22) rows in all.
Front Neck Shaping
Keep patt constant while shaping as follows:
Row 1: work patt as set, ending dc2tog over last ch sp and second ch of ch 3, turn.
Row 2: ch 1, 1 dc in next st (= dc2tog), work patt as set to end, turn.
Row 3: work patt as set, ending dc2tog over last 2 sts, turn.
Rep rows 2 and 3 a total of 4 (5, 6) more times—22 (24, 26) sts; 27 (31, 37) rows in all. Fasten off.

RIGHT FRONT
GRID PATTERN C
Row 1: ch 3, skip first 2 dc, *1 dc in next dc, ch 1, skip 1 st (which may be 1 dc or ch 1), rep from *, ending 1 dc in second ch of ch 2 at beg previous row, turn.
Row 2: ch 2, skip first dc, 1 dc in ch-1 sp, 1 dc in next dc *[ch 1, skip 1 ch, 1 dc in next dc, 1 dc in ch-1 sp, 1 dc in next dc] twice, ch 1, skip 1 ch, [1 dc in next dc, 1 dc in ch-1 sp] 4 times, 1 dc in next dc, rep from *, ending [1 dc in next dc, 1 dc in ch-1 sp] 1 (3, 5) times, 1 dc in second ch of ch 3, turn.
Rows 3–6: work as for rows 1 and 2, twice.
Row 7: ch 2, skip first dc, 1 dc in each of next 2 (6, 10) dc, *[ch 1, skip 1 ch, 1 dc in each of next 3 dc] twice, ch 1, skip 1 ch, 1 dc in each of next 9 dc, rep from *, ending 1 dc in each of next 2 dc, 1 dc in second ch of ch 2, turn.
Row 8: ch 2, skip first dc, 1 dc in each of next 2 dc, *[ch 1, skip 1 ch, 1 dc in each of next 3 dc] twice, ch 1, skip 1 ch, 1 dc in each of next 9 dc, rep from *, ending 1 dc in each of next 2 (6, 10) dc, 1 dc in second ch of ch 2, turn.
Rows 9 and 10: work as for rows 7 and 8.
These 10 rows form grid pattern C. Repeat them as given below. With size 3.00 mm hook and col A, ch 34 (38, 42).
Foundation row (RS row): 1 dc in third ch from hook, 1 dc in next ch, *[ch 1, skip 1 ch, 1 dc in each of next 3 ch,] twice, ch 1, skip 1 ch, 1 dc in each of next 9 ch, rep from *, ending 1 dc in each of

next 3 (7, 11) ch to end, turn—33 (37, 41) sts.

Beginning grid pattern C row 1 (7, 1), work 15 (17, 21) rows, ending grid pattern C row 3 (WS row)—16 (18, 22) rows in all.

Front Neck Shaping

Keep patt constant while shaping as follows:

Row 1: ch 1, 1 dc in next st (= dc2tog), work patt as set to end, turn.

Row 2: work patt as set, ending dc2tog over last 2 sts, turn.

Rep rows 1 and 2 a total of 4 (5, 6) more times and row 1 again—22 (24, 26) sts; 27 (31, 37) rows in all. Fasten off.

SLEEVES (make 2)

Sleeves are worked from top edge down to cuff.

With size 3.00 mm hook, ch 70 (78, 86).

Foundation row (RS row): 1 dc in third ch from hook, 1 dc in each of next 1 (5, 9) ch, *[ch 1, skip 1 ch, 1 dc in each of next 3 ch] twice, ch 1, skip 1 ch, 1 dc in each of next 9 ch, rep from * twice more, work [ ] twice, ch 1, skip 1 ch, 1 dc in each of next 3 (7, 11) ch to end, turn. 69 (77, 85) sts.

Beginning grid pattern A row 7 (1, 1), work 2 (4, 6) rows, ending grid pattern A row 8 (4, 6).

Sleeve Shaping

Keep patt constant while shaping as follows:

Dec row 1: ch 1, skip first dc, 1 dc in next st (= dc2tog), work patt as set, ending dc2tog over last st and second ch at beg previous row, turn—67 (75, 83) sts.

Dec row 2: ch 1, skip top of dc2tog, work patt as set, ending dc2tog over last 2 sts, turn—65 (73, 81) sts.

Rep dec row 2 a total of 14 (16, 18) more times, ending grid pattern C row 4 (2, 6). 37 (41, 45) sts—19 (23, 27) rows in all. Work 4 (6, 6) rows in patt as set—23 (29, 33) rows in all. (Adjust sleeve length here if required.) Fasten off.

FINISHING

Join shoulders for 22 (24, 26) sts at each side, matching patts. On each front, count down 17 (19, 21) rows from shoulder seam and place a marker at side edge. On back, count down 18 (20, 22) rows from shoulder seam and place a marker at each side. Join top edge of each sleeve to armhole edge between markers, matching the mesh grids exactly.

Press as instructed on yarn labels.

Weave Tartan Pattern

Lay the work on a smooth, flat surface, right side up. Begin at a vertical line of holes, next to one front edge. Cut a length of col B 4½ times longer than the line of holes. Double the thread and pass the 2 ends together through the needle eye. Bring needle up through lowest mesh hole and through the loop of col B. Now thread the needle alternately up and down through the line of holes to the neck edge. Pull gently on the work to make sure the stitches are not tight, or the weaving will distort the shape. Then weave back again, filling the gaps, to the lower edge. Pass yarn to wrong side and run in the end up the wrong side of the woven line. Work towards side edge: weave next vertical line of holes in col C, and following line in col B. Repeat colors (B, C, B) for each group of 3 lines. Lines crossing shoulder seams should be woven as one length, from lower edge to lower edge. Weave all the lines in this direction, including the lines across the sleeves.

Join the side seams (but not the sleeve seams), and then weave all the lines in the other direction in the same way to form the pattern. Join sleeve seams.

Turn-Back Cuffs (make 2)
With WS of sleeve facing and size 2.50 mm hook, join col A to base of sleeve seam.
Round 1: ch 1, 1 sc in each dc and in each ch-1 sp all round, ending 1 sl st under ch 1 at beg of round.
Round 2: ch 1, 1 sc in each sc, ending 1 sl st under ch 1 at beg of round.
Rep round 2 a total of 5 more times. 7 rounds in all.
Edging round: turn and with WS of cuff rounds facing: ch 1, 1 rsc in each sc, ending 1 sl st under ch 1 at beg of round. Fasten off.
Front, Neck, and Lower Edge Border
With size 2.50 mm hook, join col A to base of right side seam.
Round 1: ch 1, 1 sc in base of each dc and 1 sc in each ch sp, ending 3 sc in same place at corner, 2 sc in side edge of each row, ending sc2tog at first neck corner, 1 sc in each st across back neck, ending sc2tog at second neck corner, 2 sc in side edge of each row, ending 3 sc in same place at second front corner, 1 sc in base of each dc and 1 sc in each ch sp around lower edge, ending 1 sl st under ch 1 at beg of round.
Round 2: ch 1, 1 sc in each sc, with 3 sc in same place at each front corner and sc2tog at each back neck corner, ending 1 sl st under ch 1 at beg of round.

Round 3: work as for round 2, but up right front edge work: [1 sc in each of next 6 (7, 9) sc, ch 2, skip 2 ch] 4 times (complete as round 2).
Round 4: work as for round 2, working 2 sc in each ch-2 sp.
Round 5: work as for round 2.
Edging round: turn and with WS of border facing: ch 1, 1 rsc in each sc, ending 1 sl st under ch 1 at beg of round. Fasten off.
Sew on buttons to match buttonholes.
Press as instructed on yarn labels.

BERET INSTRUCTIONS

Round 1: with size 3.00 mm hook and col A, ch 6 and join into a ring with 1 sl st in first ch made.
Round 2: (work over starting end) ch 1, 12 sc into ring, 1 sl st under ch 1 at beg of round—12 sts.
Round 3: ch 2, 1 dc in st at base of ch 2, 2 dc in each of next 11 sc, 1 sl st in second ch of ch 2—24 sts.
Round 4: ch 2, 1 dc in st at base of ch 2, *1 dc in next dc, [2 dc in next dc] twice, rep from *, ending 1 dc in next dc, 2 dc in last dc, 1 sl st in second ch of ch 2—40 sts.
Round 5: ch 3, *[1 dc in next dc, ch 1, skip 1 dc] twice, 1 dc in next dc, ch 1, rep from *, ending 1 sl st in second ch of ch 3—48 sts.

BERET

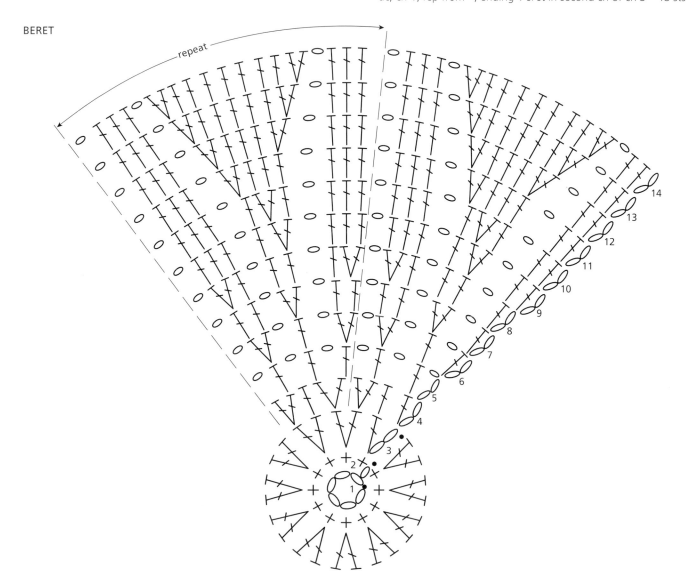

Round 6: ch 2, 1 dc in st at base of ch 2, ch 1, skip 1 ch, *1 dc in next dc, ch 1, skip 1 ch, [2 dc in next dc, ch 1, skip 1 ch] twice, rep from *, ending 2 dc in last dc, ch 1, 1 sl st in second ch of ch 3—64 sts.

Round 7: ch 2, 1 dc in next dc, *ch 1, skip 1 ch, 2 dc in next dc, [ch 1, skip 1 ch, 1 dc in each of next 2 dc] twice, rep from *, ending 1 sl st in second ch of ch 2—72 sts.

Round 8: ch 2, 1 dc in st at base of these 2 ch, 1 dc in next dc, *ch 1, skip 1 ch, 1 dc in each of next 2 dc, ch 1, skip 1 ch, 1 dc in first of 2 dc, 2 dc in next dc, ch 1, skip 1 ch, 2 dc in first of 2 dc, 1 dc in next dc, rep from *, ending ch 1, 1 sl st in second ch of ch 2—88 sts. (Check gauge here.)

Round 9: ch 2, 1 dc in each of next 2 dc, *ch 1, skip 1 ch, 2 dc in first of 2 dc, 1 dc in next dc, [ch 1, skip 1 ch, 1 dc in each of next 3 dc] twice, rep from *, ending ch 1, 1 sl st in second of 2 ch—96 sts.

Round 10: ch 2, 1 dc in each of 2 dc, *ch 1, skip 1 ch, 1 dc in next dc, 2 dc in next dc, 1 dc in next dc, [ch 1, skip 1 ch, 1 dc in each of next 3 dc] twice, rep from *, ending ch 1, 1 sl st in second of 2 ch—104 sts.

Round 11: ch 2, 1 dc in each of next 2 dc, *ch 1, skip 1 ch, 1 dc in each of next 3 dc, 2 dc in next dc, [ch 1, skip 1 ch, 1 dc in each of next 3 dc] twice, rep from *, ending ch 1, 1 sl st in second ch of ch 2—112 sts.

Round 12: ch 2, 1 dc in each of next 2 dc, *ch 1, skip 1 ch, 2 dc in first of 5 dc, 1 dc in each of next 3 dc, 2 dc in next dc, [ch 1, skip 1 ch, 1 dc in each of next 3 dc] twice, rep from *, ending 1 sl st in second ch of ch 2—128 sts.

Second and Third Sizes Only

Round 13: ch 2, 1 dc in each of next 2 dc, *ch 1, skip 1 ch, 2 dc in first of 7 dc, 1 dc in each of 5 dc, 2 dc in next dc, [ch 1, skip 1 ch, 1 dc in each of next 3 dc] twice, rep from *, ending 1 sl st in second ch of ch 2—144 sts.

Third Size Only

Round 14: ch 2, 1 dc in each of next 2 dc, *ch 1, skip 1 ch, 2 dc in first of 9 dc, 1 dc in each of next 7 dc, 2 dc in next dc, [ch 1, skip 1

ch, 1 dc in each of next 3 dc] twice, rep from *, ending 1 sl st in second ch of ch 2—160 sts.

All Sizes

128 (144, 160) sts.

Mesh round: ch 3, skip 1 st (which may be ch 1 or 1 dc), 1 dc in next dc, *ch 1, skip 1 st, 1 dc in next dc, rep from *, ending ch 1, skip 1 st, 1 sl st in second ch of ch 3.

Next round: ch 2, 1 dc in ch-1 sp, 1 dc in next dc, *ch 1, skip 1 ch, [1 dc in next dc, 1 dc in ch-1 sp] 3 (4, 5) times, 1 dc in next dc, [ch 1, skip 1 ch, 1 dc in next dc, 1 dc in ch-1 sp, 1 dc in next dc] twice, rep from *, ending ch 1, skip 1 ch, 1 sl st in second ch of ch 2.

Rep mesh round and foll round twice more.

Second and Third Sizes Only

Next round: ch 2, 1 dc in each dc and [ch 1, skip 1 ch] over each ch-1 sp, ending 1 sl st in second ch of ch 2.

Third Size Only

Rep last round once more

All Sizes

18 (20, 22) rounds in all.

Dec round: ch 2, dc2tog over next 2 dc, *ch 1, skip 1 ch, 1 dc in next dc, [dc2tog over next 2 dc] 3 (4, 5) times, [ch 1, skip 1 ch, 1 dc in next dc, dc2tog over next 2 dc] twice, ending ch 1, skip 1 ch, 1 sl st in second ch of ch 2—88 (96, 104) sts.

BORDER

Change to size 2.50 mm hook.

Round 1: ch 1, 1 sc in each st (including ch sps), ending 1 sl st under ch 1 at beg of round.

Round 2: ch 1, 1 sc in each sc, ending 1 sl st under ch 1 at beg of round.

Rep round 2 a total of 5 more times.

Edging round: turn and with WS of border facing: ch 1, 1 rsc in each sc, ending 1 sl st under ch 1 at beg of round. Fasten off.

FINISHING

Pull gently on starting end of yarn to tighten center of beret. With cols B and C, weave the pattern in the same way as the jacket, beginning at round 4 at the center of the beret and ending at the border.

With col C, make a tassel: wind yarn about 20 times around a piece of cardboard 4" wide. Pass a length of yarn under the threads at one edge of card and tie firmly, leaving ends at least 8" long. Cut through the threads at the other edge of the card (diagram 1). Tie firmly with another length of yarn, ½" from top (diagram 2). Use the long ends to sew the tassel to the center of the beret.

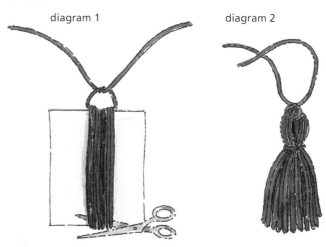

diagram 1   diagram 2

TWO-COLOR PULLOVER

THIS BOLD, BRIGHT, AND FUN PULLOVER IS GREAT TO WORK
WITH THE TECHNIQUE OF TWO-COLOR ROWS.

SIZES

APPROXIMATE AGES	1–2 yrs	3–4 yrs	5–6 yrs
to fit chest	22"	24"	26"
actual measurement	24"	26"	28"
length to shoulder	13¾"	15¼"	17¾"
sleeve seam with cuff folded back	9½"	11"	13"

MATERIALS

3 (4, 5) balls of Country Style DK by Sirdar (45% acrylic,
40% nylon, 15% wool, 50g/175yds), col A (414 Ivory
Cream) *or* comparable yarn
1 (1, 1) ball of Country Style DK by Sirdar, col B (426 Cerise)
or comparable yarn
4.00 mm and 4.50 mm hooks
2 buttons
Stitch holder

GAUGE

15½ sts and 10 rows = 4" in two-color pattern with size
4.50 mm hook

NOTE
Carry col B loosely up side edge of work between two-
color rows—no need to fasten off.

INSTRUCTIONS

BACK
With size 4.50 mm hook and col A, ch 48 (52, 56).
Foundation row: 1 sc in second ch from hook, 1 sc in each ch to
end, ch 1, turn. 47 (51, 55) sc.
Two-Color Pattern
Row 1 (WS row): with col A, ch 2 (do not count as first st), 1 hdc in
first st, 1 hdc in each st to end, turn.
Row 2: with col A, ch 2, 1 hdc in first hdc, 1 hdc in each st to end,
turn.
Row 3 (WS row): change to col B, ch 1, 1 sc in first hdc, *ch 1, skip
1 hdc, 1 sc in next hdc, rep from * to end, leave working lp on
holder. Without turning work, insert hook in first sc of B at beg of
row, pull through a lp of A, ch 1, 1 sc in same sc of B, *1 dc in hdc
of A below first ch sp (enclosing ch of B), 1 sc in next sc of B, rep
from * to end, 1 sl st in lp of B on holder, turn. Remove holder.

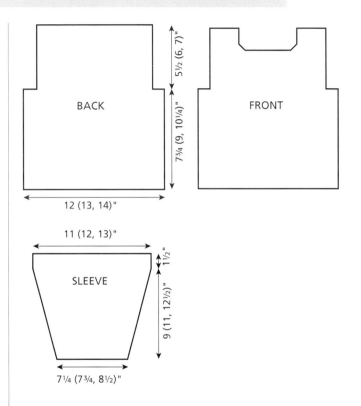

BACK

FRONT

5½ (6, 7)"

7¾ (9, 10¼)"

12 (13, 14)"

11 (12, 13)"

1½"

SLEEVE

9 (11, 12½)"

7¼ (7¾, 8½)"

TWO-COLOR PATTERN

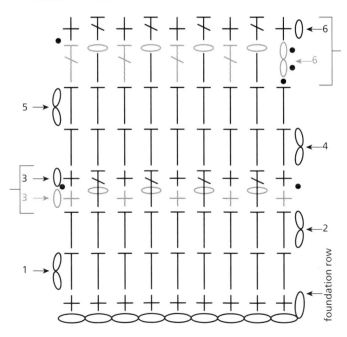

foundation row

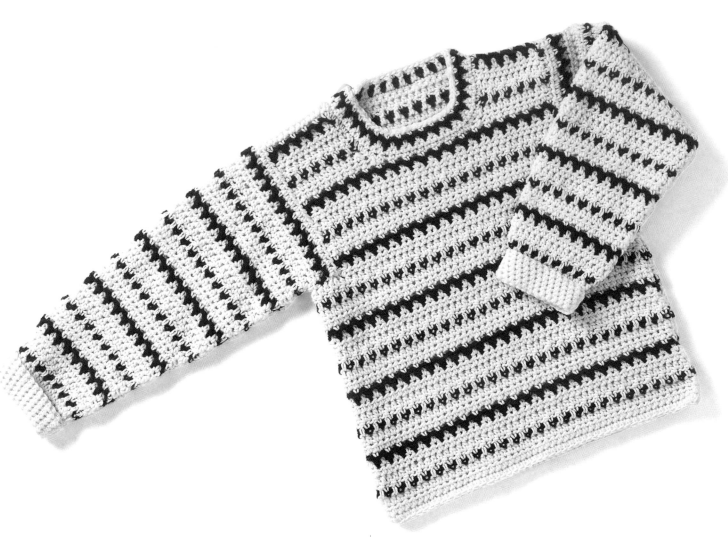

Row 4: work as for row 1.

Row 5: work as for row 2.

Row 6 (RS row): change to col B, 1 sl st in first hdc, ch 3, skip next hdc, *1 dc in next hdc, ch 1, skip 1 hdc, rep from *, ending 1 dc in last hdc, leave working lp on holder. Without turning work, insert hook in first ch of B at beg of row, pull through a lp of A, 1 sl st in next ch of B, ch 1, 1 sc in same ch of B as 1 sl st, *1 dc behind ch of B into hdc of A below, 1 sc in next dc of B, rep from * to end, 1 sl st in lp of B on holder, turn. Remove holder.

These 6 rows form the two-color pattern. Rep them 2 (2, 3) more times—19 (19, 25) rows in all.

Work patt rows 1 (1–4, 1) again—20 (23, 26) rows in all. Fasten off both cols.

Armhole Shaping

With RS (WS, RS) facing, rejoin col A to seventh hdc of last row.

Next row: ch 2, 1 hdc in same hdc, 1 hdc in each of next 34 (38, 42) hdc, turn, leaving last 6 hdc unworked—35 (39, 43) hdc. **

Beg patt row 3 (6, 3), work 13 (14, 17) more patt rows, ending patt row 3 (1, 1). Fasten off.

FRONT

Work as for back to **.

Beg patt row 3 (6, 3), work 7 (7, 10) more patt rows, ending patt row 3 (6, 6).

Neck Shaping

First Side

Row 1: with A, ch 2, 1 hdc in first st, 1 hdc in each of next 8 (10, 10) sts, hdc2tog over next 2 sts, turn—10 (12, 12) sts.

Row 2: ch 2, hdc2tog over hdc2tog and next hdc, 1 hdc in each hdc to end, turn—9 (11, 11) sts.

Beg patt row 6 (3, 3), work 4 (5, 5) more rows, ending patt row 3 (1, 1). Fasten off.

Second Side

With RS (WS, WS) facing, leave 12 (12, 16) sts at center front and rejoin col A to next st.

Row 1: ch 2, hdc2tog over next 2 sts, 1 hdc in each st to end, turn—10 (12, 12) sts.

Row 2: ch 2, 1 hdc in first hdc, 1 hdc in each of next 7 (9, 9) hdc, hdc2tog over last hdc and hdc2tog, turn—9 (11, 11) sts.

Beg patt row 6 (3, 3), work 4 (5, 5) more rows, ending patt row 3 (1, 1). Fasten off.

SLEEVES (make 2)

With size 4.50 mm hook and col A, ch 30 (32, 34).

Work foundation row as for back—29 (31, 33) sc.

Sleeve Shaping

Inc row 1: with A, ch 2, 2 hdc in first st, 1 hdc in each st to end, turn.

Inc row 2: with A, ch 2, 2 hdc in first hdc, 1 hdc in each hdc to end, turn.

Inc row 3: work as for row 3 of two-color pattern.

Inc rows 4 and 5: work as for inc rows 1 and 2.

Inc row 6: work as for row 6 of two-color pattern—33 (35, 37) sts.

Rep these 6 rows a total of 2 (3, 3) more times.

First and Third Sizes Only
Work inc rows 1 and 2 again.
All Sizes
43 (47, 51) sts. 21 (25, 27) rows in all, ending inc row 2 (6, 2). Beg patt row 3 (1, 3), work in two-color pattern until sleeve measures 9 (10½, 12½)" in all.
Place a marker at each end of last row. Work 4 more patt rows. Fasten off.

NECK BAND
Join left shoulder seam. With RS facing and size 4.00 mm hook, join col A at armhole edge of right shoulder on back.

Row 1: ch 1, 1 sc in first st, 1 sc in each st along top of back to shoulder seam, sc2tog at corner, 10 (12, 12) sc down side edge of first side of front neck shaping, sc2tog at corner, 1 sc in each st along center front, sc2tog at corner, 10 (12, 12) sc up side edge of front neck shaping to corner, turn.

Row 2: ch 1, 1 sc in first sc, 1 sc in each sc to last 9 (11, 11) sc, turn, leaving last 9 (11, 11) sc to form edging of back shoulder. (Count number of sc on this row: there should be an odd number; if not, work sc2tog at center back.)

Row 3: change to col B, 1 sl st in first sc, ch 3, skip next sc, *1 dc in next sc, ch 1, skip 1 sc, rep from *, ending 1 dc in last sc, leave working lp on holder. Without turning work, insert hook in first ch of B at beg of row, pull through a lp of A, 1 sl st in next ch of B, ch 1, 1 sc in same ch of B as 1 sl st, *1 dc behind ch of B into sc of A below, 1 sc in next dc of B, rep from * to end, 1 sl st in lp of B from holder, turn. Remove holder.

Row 4: ch 1, 1 sl st in each st to end. Fasten off.

BUTTONHOLE BAND
With RS facing and size 4.00 mm hook, join col A to corner of neck band at left front shoulder.

Row 1: ch 1, 5 sc in side edge of neck band, 1 sc in each of next 9 (11, 11) hdc along shoulder edge, turn—14 (16, 16) sc.

Row 2: ch 1, 1 sc in first sc, 1 sc in each of next 2 sc, [ch 2, skip 2 sc, 1 sc in each of next 2 (3, 3) sc] twice, ch 2, skip 2 sc, 1 sc in last sc, turn.

Row 3: ch 1, 1 sc in first sc, 2 sc in each ch sp and 1 sc in each sc to end. Fasten off.

FINISHING
Place buttonhole band over back, matching edges of last rows of back and front, and sew down side edge of buttonhole band at armhole edge.
Join top edges of sleeves to armhole edges, with sleeve rows above markers matching armhole shapings.
Join side and sleeve seams, matching patt rows.

Cuffs (make 2)
With RS of sleeve facing and size 4.00 mm hook, join col A at base of sleeve seam.

Round 1: ch 1, 1 sc in base of each of 29 (31, 33) ch, 1 sl st in first sc of round.

Round 2: ch 1, 1 sc in each of first 3 (3, 4) sc, [sc2tog over next 2 sc, 1 sc in each of next 3 (4, 4) sc] 4 times, sc2tog over next 2 sc, 1 sc in each sc, ending 1 sc in first sc of round—5 decs made.

Round 3: 1 sc in each sc, ending 1 sc in first sc of round.
Rep round 3 a total of 6 more times. Fasten off.

Lower Edge
With RS facing and size 4.00 mm hook, join col A at base of one side seam in sp between 2 sc of first row.

Round 1: ch 1, 1 sc in same sp, 1 sc in each sp between 2 sc of first row all round, ending 1 sl st in first sc of round. Fasten off.
Sew on buttons to match buttonholes.
Press as instructed on yarn labels.

TWO HATS

ONE BASIC PATTERN MAKES TWO DESIGNS: ADD EARS, FACE, AND TAIL FOR A FRIENDLY RABBIT HAT, OR ADD THE STALK AND FRUIT TRIM FOR A FRUIT HAT.

SIZES

to fit head   18"   19"   20"

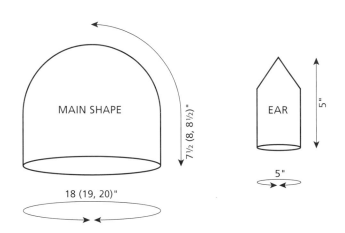

MAIN SHAPE

7½ (8, 8½)"

18 (19, 20)"

EAR

5"

5"

RABBIT HAT INSTRUCTIONS

MAIN SHAPE

Round 1: with size 3.00 mm hook and col A, ch 6 and join into a ring with 1 sl st in first ch made.
Round 2: (work over starting end): ch 1, 12 sc into ring, 1 sl st in first sc of round—12 sts.
Round 3: ch 1, 1 sc in st at base of this ch, [1 sc in next sc, 2 sc in next sc] 5 times, 1 sc in next sc, 1 sl st in ch 1 at beg of round—18 sts.
Round 4: ch 1, 1 sc in st at base of this ch, [1 sc in each of next 2 sc, 2 sc in next sc] 5 times, 1 sc in each of next 2 sc, 1 sl st in ch 1 at beg of round—24 sts.
Round 5: ch 1, 1 sc in st at base of this ch, [1 sc in each of next 3 sc, 2 sc in next sc] 5 times, 1 sc in each of next 3 sc, 1 sl st in ch 1 at beg of round—30 sts.
Round 6: ch 1, 1 sc in st at base of this ch, [1 sc in each of next 4 sc, 2 sc in next sc] 5 times, 1 sc in each of next 4 sc, 1 sl st in ch 1 at beg of round—36 sts.
Round 7: ch 1, 1 sc in st at base of this ch, [1 sc in each of next 5 sc, 2 sc in next sc] 5 times, 1 sc in each of next 5 sc, 1 sl st in ch 1 at beg of round—42 sts.
Round 8: ch 1, 1 sc in st at base of this ch, [1 sc in each of next 6 sc, 2 sc in next sc] 5 times, 1 sc in each of next 6 sc, 1 sl st in ch 1 at beg of round—48 sts.
Round 9: ch 1, 1 sc in st at base of this ch, [1 sc in each of next 7 sc, 2 sc in next sc] 5 times, 1 sc in each of next 7 sc, 1 sl st in ch 1 at beg of round—54 sts.

MATERIALS

RABBIT HAT
2 (2, 2) balls of Matchmaker Merino 4-ply by Jaeger (100% wool, 50g/200yds), col A (782 Flannel) *or* comparable yarn
Scraps of black and white DK or 4-ply wool
3.00 mm hook
6" x 6" square of polyester batting
Blunt-ended tapestry needle for embroidery
Darning needle
Thin cardstock
FRUIT HAT
1 (2, 2) balls Matchmaker Merino 4-ply by Jaeger (100% wool, 50g/200yds), col A (715 Thyme) *or* comparable yarn
Small ball of Matchmaker Merino 4-ply by Jaeger, col B (713 Meadow) *or* comparable yarn
Scrap of Matchmaker Merino 4-ply by Jaeger, col C (697 Peony) *or* comparable yarn
3.00 mm hook

GAUGE

First 13 rounds = 4" in diameter with 3.00 mm hook

ROUNDS 1–5

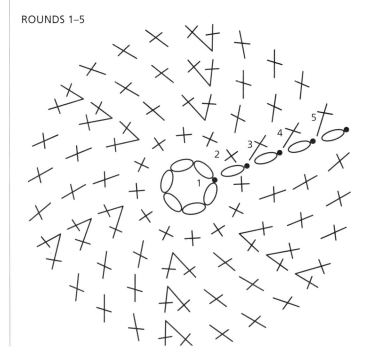

Round 10: ch 1, 1 sc in st at base of this ch, [1 sc in each of next 8 sc, 2 sc in next sc] 5 times, 1 sc in each of next 8 sc, 1 sl st in ch 1 at beg of round—60 sts.

Round 11: ch 1, 1 sc in st at base of this ch, [1 sc in each of next 9 sc, 2 sc in next sc] 5 times, 1 sc in each of next 9 sc, 1 sl st in ch 1 at beg of round—66 sts.

Round 12: ch 1, 1 sc in st at base of this ch, [1 sc in each of next 10 sc, 2 sc in next sc] 5 times, 1 sc in each of next 10 sc, 1 sl st in ch 1 at beg of round—72 sts.

Round 13: ch 1, 1 sc in st at base of this ch, [1 sc in each of next 11 sc, 2 sc in next sc] 5 times, 1 sc in each of next 11 sc, 1 sl st in ch 1 at beg of round—78 sts. (Check gauge here.)

Round 14: ch 1, 1 sc in st at base of this ch, [1 sc in each of next 12 sc, 2 sc in next sc] 5 times, 1 sc in each of next 12 sc, 1 sl st in ch 1 at beg of round—84 sts.

Round 15: ch 1, 1 sc in st at base of this ch, [1 sc in each of next 13 sc, 2 sc in next sc] 5 times, 1 sc in each of next 13 sc, 1 sl st in ch 1 at beg of round—90 sts.

Round 16: ch 1, 1 sc in st at base of this ch, [1 sc in each of next 14 sc, 2 sc in next sc] 5 times, 1 sc in each of next 14 sc, 1 sl st in ch 1 at beg of round—96 sts.

Round 17: ch 1, 1 sc in st at base of this ch, [1 sc in each of next 15 sc, 2 sc in next sc] 5 times, 1 sc in each of next 15 sc, 1 sl st in ch 1 at beg of round—102 sts.

Second and Third Sizes Only

Round 18: ch 1, 1 sc in st at base of this ch, [1 sc in each of next 16 sc, 2 sc in next sc] 5 times, 1 sc in each of next 16 sc, 1 sl st in ch 1 at beg of round—108 sts.

Third Size Only

Round 19: ch 1, 1 sc in st at base of this ch, [1 sc in each of next 17 sc, 2 sc in next sc] 5 times, 1 sc in each of next 17 sc, 1 sl st in ch 1 at beg of round—114 sts.

diagram 1

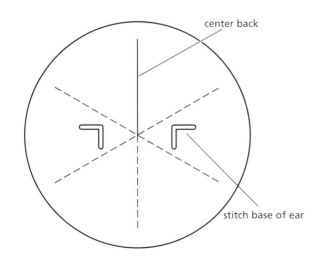

center back

stitch base of ear

diagram 2

All Sizes

102 (108, 114) sts.

Plain round: ch 1, 1 sc in st at base of this ch, 1 sc in each sc to last sc, skip last sc, 1 sl st in ch 1 at beg of round.

Rep this round until hat measures 6 (6½, 7)" from center to outside edge, ending with a complete round.

Dec round: ch 1, skip 1 sc at base of this ch, [1 sc in each of next 15 (16, 17) sc, sc2tog over next 2 sc] 5 times, 1 sc in each of next 15 (16, 17) sc, 1 sl st in ch 1 at beg of round   96 (102, 108) sts.

Rep plain round until hat measures 7½ (8, 8½)" from center to outside edge, ending with a complete round. Fasten off.

Allow lower edge to roll toward right side of work.

EARS (make 2)

Round 1: With size 3.00 mm hook and col A, ch 30 and join into a ring with 1 sl st in first ch made.

Round 2: ch 1, 1 sc in ch at base of this ch, 1 sc in each ch to last ch, skip last ch, 1 sl st in ch 1 at beg of round—30 sts.

Round 3: ch 1, 1 sc in st at base of this ch, 1 sc in each sc to last sc, skip last sc, 1 sl st in ch 1 at beg of round.

Rep round 3 a total of 15 more times—18 rounds.

Dec round: ch 1, skip st at base of this ch, 1 sc in each sc to last 3 sc, sc2tog over next 2 sc, skip last sc, 1 sl st in ch 1 at beg of round—28 sts.

Next round: ch 1, 1 sc in st at base of this ch, 1 sc in each sc to sc2tog, skip this last st, 1 sl st in ch 1 at beg of round.

Rep these 2 rounds twice more—24 sts.

Rep dec round a total of 9 more times—6 sts. Fasten off.

diagram 3

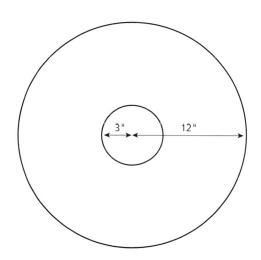

FINISHING

Press ears flat with shaping at center front. Cut a piece of batting to same shape as each ear, slip inside ears. With col A and darning needle, work a line of chain st (as page 12) down the center of each ear to cover the shaping line, catching down to the batting but not through to the back of the ear. Slip stitch along the base of each ear to enclose the batting. Fold the base to form a right angle and sew to top of hat as indicated in diagram 1. (You may find it helpful to stretch the hat over a bowl or child's ball.)

Use black yarn to embroider features as shown in diagram 2.

Use a compass to draw diagram 3 twice on thin cardstock. Use white yarn to make a pompon as described on page 108 (Nursery Pillow). Sew pompon at center back.

FRUIT HAT INSTRUCTIONS

With col A, work main shape as for rabbit hat.

FRUIT TRIM
Fruit Chain
With size 3.00 mm hook and col C, ch 9.
Round 1: tr7tog in fourth ch from hook, [9 ch, tr7tog in fourth ch from hook] twice, join into a ring with 1 sl st in first ch made. Fasten off.

Stalk
With size 3.00 mm hook and col B, ch 10.
Row 1: 1 sc in second ch from hook, 1 sc in each of next 8 ch, turn—9 sc.
Row 2: ch 1, 1 sc in first sc, 1 sc in each sc to end, turn.
Rep row 2 a total of 4 more times. 6 rows.
Next row: fold lower edge up to meet top edge and work through both thicknesses to form a tube: ch 1, [1 sl st through both thicknesses] 9 times.
Cont in rounds:
Round 1: ch 1, 6 sc evenly spaced around end of tube (inserting hook from outside of tube through to inside), ending 1 sl st in first sc of round.
Round 2: ch 1, 1 sc in sc at base of this ch, 2 sc in each of next 5 sc, 1 sl st in ch 1 at beg of round—12 sts.
Round 3: ch 1, 1 sc in sc at base of this ch, [1 sc in next sc, 2 sc in next sc] 5 times, 1 sc in last sc, 1 sl st in ch 1 at

beg of round—18 sts.
Slip fruit chain over stalk.
Round 4: ch 1, 1 sc in sc at base of this ch tog with first ch sp of fruit chain, [1 sc in each of next 2 sc, 2 sc in next sc, 1 sc in each of next 2 sc] all tog with same ch sp of fruit chain, *push fruit bobble to RS of work, [2 sc in next sc, 1 sc in each of next 2 sc] tog with next ch sp of fruit chain, twice; rep from * once more, push fruit bobble to RS of work, 1 sl st in ch 1 at beg of round—24 sts.
First Leaf
Row 1: ch 1, 1 sc in sc at base of this ch, 1 sc in each of next 2 sc, 2 sc in next sc, turn—5 sc.
Row 2: ch 1, 1 sc in each of first 4 sc, 2 sc in last sc, turn—6 sc.
Row 3: ch 1, 1 sc in first sc, 1 sc in each sc to end, turn.
Rep row 3 a total of 7 more times—10 rows.
Row 11: ch 1, skip first sc, 1 sc in each sc to end, turn—5 sc.
Rep row 11 a total of 3 more times—2 sc.
Row 15: ch 1, skip first sc, 1 sc in last sc—1 st. Fasten off.
Second Leaf
With RS of trim facing, rejoin col B to next sc of round 4. Work as for first leaf.
Work 4 more leaves in the same way, without fastening off last leaf.
Edging round: ch 1, *1 sc in side edge of each row of leaf, sc3tog at inner corner, 1 sc in side edge of each row of next leaf, 4 sc in same place at outer point, rep from * all around edge of trim, ending 1 sl st in ch 1 at beg of round. Fasten off.
Sew fruit trim to center top of hat, spreading the leaves evenly. Use col B to backstitch all around the edge of the trim.

CHRISTENING SHAWL

WARM, LIGHT, AND SMOOTH TO THE TOUCH, PURE SILK YARN MAKES
THIS SHAWL A FAMILY HEIRLOOM.

SIZE

approx. 43" x 43"

MATERIALS

2 cones of undyed 2-ply silk yarn by Texere Yarns (100%
silk, 150g cones) (ref.SS16) *or* comparable yarn
2.50 mm hook

GAUGE

Work Center Square, ending round 4. Press as instructed
on yarn label. Square should measure 2¼" in each
direction. If your square is too small, try again with a
larger hook; if it is too large, try a smaller hook.
Gauge is not crucial provided a change in finished size is
acceptable. However, if your gauge is too tight, the shawl
may feel too firm, and if your gauge is too loose, the
shawl may not hold its shape and extra yarn may be
required.

Special Abbreviation: 1 fan 1 tr, 4 dc in base lp of this tr,
inserting hook behind 2 threads.

This design is worked in rounds, beginning at center of shawl.

CENTER SQUARE

With size 2.50 mm hook, ch 6 and join into a ring with 1 sl st in first
ch made.
Round 1: ch 1, 12 sc into ring and over starting end of yarn, 1 sl st
under ch 1 at beg of round.
Round 2: ch 3, 1 dc in same place as base of 3 ch, 2 dc in each of
rem 11 sc, ending 1 sl st in third ch of ch 3 at beg of round—24 sts.
Round 3: ch 3, tr2tog in each of next 2 dc, *ch 3, [dc3tog, inserting
hook in same place as last st and in each of next 2 dc, ch 3] twice,
tr3tog, inserting hook in same place as last st and in each of next 2
dc, rep from * twice more, ch 3, dc3tog, inserting hook as before,
ch 3, dc3tog, inserting hook in same place as last st, in next dc and
in st at base of ch 3 at beg of round, ch 3, 1 sl st in top of tr2tog.

Round 4: ch 4, 1 sl st in top of tr2tog at base of ch (first picot made), *3 sc in ch-3 sp, 1 sc in top of next group, ch 3, 1 sl st in same place as last sc (second picot made), rep from *, ending 1 sl st in first ch of ch 4 at beg of round. (Check your gauge here.)

Round 5: 1 sc in corner picot, *ch 5, 1 sc in same corner picot, ch 5, 1 sc in next picot, ch 3, 1 sc in next picot, ch 5, 1 sc in next corner picot, rep from *, ending 1 sl st in sc at beg of round.

Round 6 (fan pattern): [1 sc, ch 3, 1 fan] in corner ch sp, *5 dc in third ch of next ch 5, 5 dc in second ch of next ch 3, 5 dc in third ch of next ch 5, 2 fans in corner ch sp, rep from *, ending 4 dc in 1 sc at beg of round, 1 sl st in third ch of ch 3.

Round 7: [1 sc, ch 3, 1 fan] in corner sp before next fan, *skip 1 fan, [1 fan in sp before next 5 dc, skip 5 dc] 3 times, 1 fan in sp before next fan, skip 1 fan, 2 fans in corner sp, rep from *, ending 4 dc in 1 sc at beg of round, 1 sl st in third ch of ch 3. 6 fans on each side of square.

Round 8: [1 sc, ch 3, 1 fan] in sp before next fan, *[skip 1 fan, 1 fan in sp before next fan] to corner, 2 fans in corner sp, rep from *, ending 4 dc in 1 sc at beg of round, 1 sl st in third ch of ch 3. 8 fans on each side of square.

Rep round 8 a total of 8 more times. 24 fans on each side of square. Fasten off.

CENTER SQUARE rounds 1–7

FAN MESH PATTERN

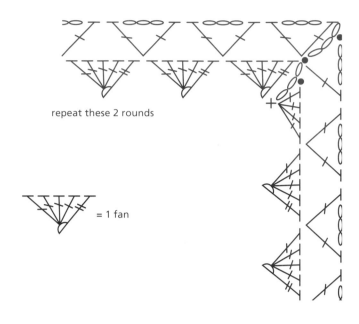

repeat these 2 rounds

= 1 fan

FIRST BAND OF SQUARES
First Square
Work as for center square rounds 1–3.
Round 4: work as for round 4 of center square, but joining third side to last round of fan pattern as follows: (hold both pieces with right sides up) at third corner, instead of 3 ch picot, work [ch 1, 1 sl st between 2 corner fans, inserting hook from WS through to RS, ch 1], *instead of next 3 ch picot, work [ch 1, 1 sl st between next 2 fans along side edge, inserting hook as before, ch 1], rep from * once, work fourth corner as third, then complete the round as set, ending 1 sl st in first ch of ch 4. Fasten off.

Second Square
Work as for first square, but join second corner to first corner of previous square, second side to fourth side of previous square, third corner to same sp as fourth corner of previous square, and third side to last row of fan pattern, working clockwise round the edge of the main piece.
Work 34 more squares in the same way, joining them as shown on general layout diagram. Note that corner squares will be joined to two squares along two adjacent sides and to center section at one corner only.

FAN MESH PATTERN
Round 1: With RS facing, rejoin yarn to picot at one corner, ch 4, 1 sl st in same picot, *ch 5, 1 sc in next picot, ch 3, 1 sc in next picot, ch 5, sc2tog over 2 joined picots, [rep from *, ending (1 sc, ch 3, 1 sc) in

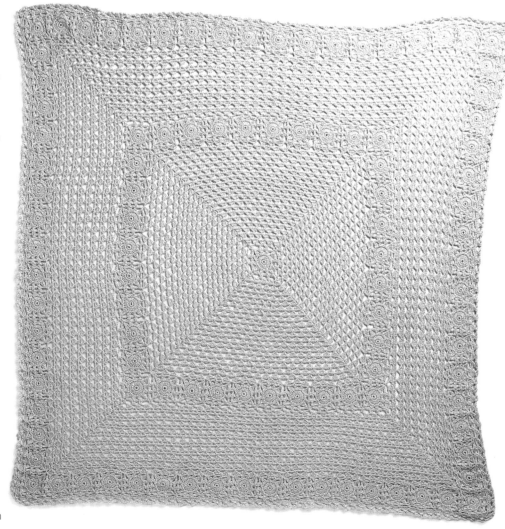

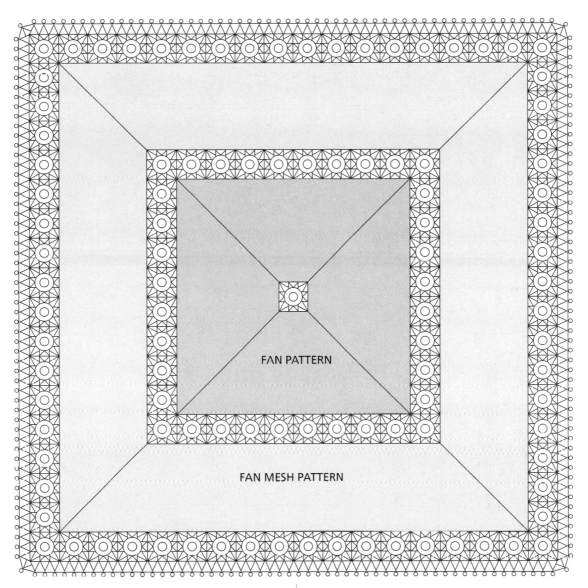

FAN PATTERN

FAN MESH PATTERN

corner picot] 3 times, rep from * along fourth side, ending 1 sl st in first ch of ch 4 at beg of round.

Round 2: [1 sc, ch 3, 1 fan] in corner sp before next fan, *skip 1 fan, [1 fan in sp before next 5 dc, skip 5 dc] 3 times, 1 fan in sp before next fan, skip 1 fan, 2 fans in corner sp, rep from *, ending 4 dc in 1 sc at beg of round, 1 sl st in third ch of ch 3.

Round 3: ch 3, [1 dc, ch 3, 1 dc] in corner sp, *skip 5 dc, [1 dc, ch 3, 1 dc] in sp before next 5 dc, [rep from *, ending (1 dc, ch 3, 1 dc) twice in corner sp] 3 times, rep from * along fourth side, ending 1 dc in first corner sp, ch 3, 1 sl st in third ch of ch 3 at beg of round.

Round 4: 1 sc in sp before next dc, ch 3, 1 fan in same corner sp, *skip [1 dc, ch 3, 1 dc], 1 fan in sp before next group, [rep from *, ending 2 fans in corner sp] 3 times, rep from * along fourth side, ending 4 dc in sc at beg of round, 1 sl st in third ch of ch 3 at beg of round.

Round 5: 1 sl st in corner sp, ch 3, [1 dc, ch 3, 1 dc] in same corner sp, *skip 1 fan, [1 dc, ch 3, 1 dc] in sp before next fan, [rep from *, ending (1 dc, ch 3, 1 dc) in corner sp] 3 times, rep from * along fourth side, ending 1 dc in first corner sp, ch 3, 1 sl st in third ch of ch 3 at beg of round.

Rep rounds 4 and 5 a total of 6 more times, and round 4 again—48 fans on each side of square.

SECOND BAND OF SQUARES
Work as for first band of squares, making 68 squares in all.

BORDER
With RS facing, rejoin yarn to one corner picot.

Border round 1: work as for round 1 of fan mesh pattern.

Border round 2: [1 sc, ch 3, 1 sc] in corner ch sp, skip 1 sc, *[5 sc in ch-5 sp, 1 sc in next sc, 3 sc in ch-3 sp, 1 sc in sc, 5 sc in ch-5 sp, skip sc2tog] to next corner, ending skip 1 sc, [1 sc, ch 3, 1 sc] in corner ch sp, rep from * 3 more times, ending skip 1 sc, 1 sl st in first sc of round.

Border round 3: ch 3, dc4tog (working first 3 sts in corner ch sp and fourth st in next sc), ch 3, 1 sl st in top of last dc4tog, ch 4, *[dc5tog over next 5 sc, ch 3, 1 sl st in top of last dc5tog, ch 4] to next corner, ending dc5tog (working first st in next sc, next 3 sts in corner ch sp and fifth st in next sc), ch 3, 1 sl st in top of last dc5tog, ch 4, rep from * 3 more times, ending 1 sl st in top of dc4tog at beg of round.

Border round 4: 1 sc in corner picot, *3 sc in same picot, sc2tog over same picot and next ch sp, 2 sc in same ch sp, sc2tog over same ch sp and next picot, rep from *, ending 1 sl st in first sc of round. Fasten off.

Press as instructed on yarn label.

GIRAFFE AND ZEBRA

MAKE THESE CUDDLY TOYS WITH ODD BALLS OF YARN.

SIZES

GIRAFFE	approx. height	12¼"
ZEBRA	approx. height	8½"

MATERIALS

GIRAFFE
1 ball of Knit 'n Save DK by Patons (100g), col A (7730 Melon) *or* comparable yarn
Scraps of Knit 'n Save DK by Patons, col B (7814 Black) *or* comparable yarn
3.50 mm hook
Polyester stuffing

ZEBRA
1 ball of Knit 'n Save DK by Patons (100g), col A (7814 Black) *or* comparable yarn
1 ball of Knit 'n Save DK by Patons, col B (7813 Snow White) *or* comparable yarn
Scraps of Knit 'n Save DK by Patons, col C (7796 Orange) *or* comparable yarn
3.50 mm hook
Polyester stuffing

GAUGE

20 sts and 20 rows = 4" in rows of sc with size 3.50 mm hook
Gauge is not crucial provided a change in size is acceptable. However, if your gauge is too loose, the toy will not hold its shape.

NOTE

Instructions are for DK yarn, but you can use a finer or heavier yarn if you wish, changing the hook size accordingly. The crochet fabric should be firm. (Changing the yarn and hook will alter the finished size.)

GIRAFFE INSTRUCTIONS

SIDE OF BODY (make 2)
Begin at back leg. With size 3.50 mm hook and col A, ch 23.
Foundation row: 1 sc in second ch from hook, 1 sc in each ch to end, turn—22 sc.
Row 2: ch 3, 1 sc in second ch from hook, 1 sc in next ch, 1 sc in each sc to end, turn—24 sc.
Row 3: ch 1, 1 sc in each of next 23 sc, 2 sc in last sc, turn—25 sc.
Row 4: ch 1, 2 sc in first sc, 1 sc in each of next 24 sc, turn—26 sc.
Row 5: ch 1, 2 sc in first sc, 1 sc in each of next 24 sc, 2 sc in last sc, turn—28 sc.

Row 6: ch 1, 1 sc in first sc, 1 sc in each sc to end, turn.
Row 7: ch 1, 1 sc in each of next 27 sc, 2 sc in last sc, turn—29 sc.
Row 8: work as for row 6.

Back Leg Shaping
Row 9: ch 1, 1 sc in each of first 4 sc, 1 sl st in next sc, fasten off. Leave next 6 sc, rejoin yarn to next sc, 1 sc in each of next 16 sc, 2 sc in last sc, turn.
Row 10: work as for row 6—18 sc.
Row 11: ch 1, sc2tog over first 2 sc, 1 sc in each of next 15 sc, 2 sc in last sc, turn—18 sts.
Row 12: work as for row 6.
Rows 13–18: rep rows 11 and 12 a total of 3 times.

Front Leg
Row 19: ch 17, 1 sc in second ch from hook, 1 sc in each of next 15 ch, 1 sc in each of next 17 sc, 2 sc in last sc, turn—35 sc.
Row 20: work as for row 6.
Row 21: ch 1, 1 sc in each of next 34 sc, 2 sc in last sc, turn—36 sc.
Row 22: ch 1, 2 sc in first sc, 1 sc in each of next 35 sc to end, turn—37 sc.
Row 23: ch 1, 2 sc in first sc, 1 sc in each of next 35 sc, 2 sc in last sc, turn—39 sc.
Row 24: ch 1, 2 sc in first sc, 1 sc in each of next 38 sc to end, turn—40 sc.
Row 25: ch 1, 1 sc in each of next 39 sc, 2 sc in last sc, turn—41 sc.

Row 26: ch 1, 2 sc in first sc, 1 sc in each of next 40 sc to end, turn—42 sc.

Front Leg Shaping

Row 27: ch 1, 1 sc in each of first 4 sc, 1 sl st in next sc, fasten off. Leave next 14 sc, rejoin yarn to next sc, 1 sc in each of next 21 sc, 2 sc in last sc, turn.

Row 28: ch 1, 2 sc in first sc, 1 sc in each of next 18 sc, turn, leaving last 4 sc unworked—20 sc.

Row 29: skip first sc, 1 sl st in next sc, 1 sc in each sc to last sc, 2 sc in last sc, turn—19 sc.

Row 30: ch 1, 2 sc in first sc, 1 sc in each sc to last 3 sc, turn—17 sc.

Row 31: work as for row 29—16 sc.

Row 32: ch 1, 2 sc in first sc, 1 sc in each sc to last 2 sc, turn—15 sc.

Rows 33 and 34: work as for rows 31 and 32—13 sc.

Row 35: skip first sc, 1 sl st in next sc, 1 sc in each sc to end, turn—11 sc.

Row 36: ch 1, 2 sc in first sc, 1 sc in each sc to last 2 sc, turn—10 sc.

Head Shaping

Row 37: ch 1, 2 sc in first sc, 1 sc in each sc to end, turn—11 sc.

Row 38: ch 1, 1 sc in each sc to last sc, 2 sc in last sc, turn—12 sc.

Rows 39 and 40: work as for rows 37 and 38—14 sc.

Row 41: ch 1, 1 sc in each of 12 sc, sc2tog over last 2 sc, turn—13 sts.

Row 42: ch 4, 1 sc in second ch from hook, 1 sc in each of next 2 ch (these 3 sc form the horn), sc2tog over next 2 sc, 1 sc in each of next 3 sc, sc2tog over next 2 sc. Fasten off.

HEAD GUSSET

With size 3.50 mm hook and col A, ch 2.

Row 1: 2 sc in second ch from hook, turn.

Row 2: ch 1, 1 sc in first sc, 2 sc in last sc, turn—3 sc.

Row 3: ch 1, 1 sc in each sc, turn.

Rows 4–6: work as for row 3.

Row 7: ch 1, 2 sc in first sc, 1 sc in next sc, 2 sc in last sc, turn—5 sc.

Row 8: ch 1, 2 sc in first sc, 1 sc in each of next 3 sc, 2 sc in last sc, turn—7 sc.

Rows 9–12: work as for row 3.

Row 13: ch 1, sc2tog over first 2 sc, 1 sc in each of next 3 sc, sc2tog over last 2 sc, turn—5 sts.

Row 14: ch 1, 1 sc in each st to end, turn.

Row 15: ch 1, sc2tog over first 2 sc, 1 sc in next sc, sc2tog over last 2 sc, turn—3 sts.

Row 16: work as for row 14.

Row 17: ch 1, sc2tog over first 2 sc, 1 sc in last sc, turn—2 sts.

Row 18: ch 1, sc2tog over rem 2 sts. Fasten off.

UNDERBODY

With size 3.50 mm hook and col A, ch 3.

Row 1: 1 sc in second ch from hook, 1 sc in next ch, turn—2 sc.

Row 2: ch 1, 1 sc in each sc, turn.

Row 3: 2 sc in first sc, 1 sc in last sc, turn—3 sc.

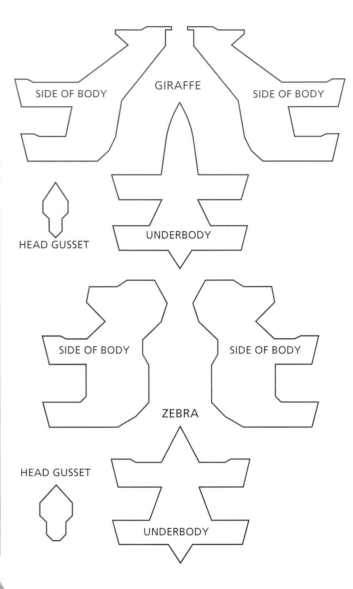

Row 4: ch 1, 2 sc in first sc, 1 sc in each sc to end, turn—4 sc.

Rows 5 and 6: work as for row 4. 6 sc.

Row 7: 17 ch, 1 sc in second ch from hook, 1 sc in each of next 15 ch, 1 sc in each sc to end, turn—22 sc.

Row 8: work as for row 7—38 sc.

Row 9: ch 1, 1 sc in first sc, 1 sc in each sc to end, turn.

Row 10: work as for row 9.

Row 11: ch 1, 2 sc in first sc, 1 sc in each sc to end, turn—39 sc.

Row 12: work as for row 11. 40 sc.

Rows 13–15: work as for row 9.

Back Leg Shaping

Row 16: ch 1, 1 sc in each of first 28 sc, turn, leaving 12 sc unworked.

Row 17: ch 1, sc2tog over first 2 sc, 1 sc in each of next 14 sc, turn, leaving 12 sc unworked.

Row 18: ch 1, sc2tog over first 2 sc, 1 sc in each sc to end, turn—14 sts.

Rows 19–24: work as for row 18—8 sts.

Rows 25 and 26: work as for row 9.

Front Legs

Rows 27 and 28: work as for row 7—40 sc.

Rows 29 and 30: work as for row 9.

Rows 31–34: work as for row 11—44 sc.

Row 35: work as for row 9.

Front Leg Shaping

Row 36: ch 1, 1 sc in each of first 28 sc, turn leaving 16 sc unworked.

Row 37: ch 1, 1 sc in each of first 12 sc, turn leaving 16 sc unworked.

Rows 38 and 39: work as for row 18—10 sts.

Rows 40–43: work as for row 9.
Rep rows 38–43 once more—8 sts.
Rep rows 38–41 twice—4 sts.
Rep rows 38 and 39 again—2 sts.

Last row: ch 1, sc2tog over 2 rem sts. Fasten off.

EARS (make 2)

With size 3.50 mm hook and col A, ch 5.

Row 1: 1 sc in second ch from hook, 1 sc in each ch to end, turn—4 sc.

Row 2: ch 1, 1 sc in first sc, 1 sc in each sc to end, turn.

Row 3: work as for row 2.

Row 4: ch 1, 1 sc in first sc, sc2tog over next 2 sc, 1 sc in last sc, turn—3 sts.

Row 5: ch 1, sc2tog over first 2 sc, 1 sc in last sc, turn—2 sts.

Row 6: ch 1, sc2tog over 2 rem sts. Fasten off.

FINISHING

Join head gusset to sides of head, matching lower point to end of nose. Leave horns protruding from top of head. Join center back seam from top of head down to tail position, leaving an opening of about 4" at center to insert polyester stuffing. Join from point of nose to corner beneath chin. Sew on underbody with lower (short) point at end of center back seam and upper (long) point beneath chin, matching sides of legs and gathering slightly across ends of feet.

Insert polyester stuffing. Push stuffing into head and down to ends of legs with the blunt end of a pencil or similar tool. The toy should be filled firmly. The firmer the stuffing, the better the giraffe will stand up. Close opening.

Sew ears to top of head, folding lower edge of each at an angle so ears stand up.

Embroidery

With col B, embroider circles of chain stitch following the photograph as a guide. Embroider a little smile in chain stitch, as illustrated.

Eyes

Bring col B out at required position and secure with a small back stitch, then take several firm stitches through the head from one eye position to the other, pulling tightly to shape the head. Then work a French knot for each eye.

Tail

Cut 6 strands col B, 19½" long, and thread them through seam at tail position, making 12 strands of equal length. Divide the strands into 3 groups of 4 and braid tightly for about 1¾", then tie an overhand knot. Trim ends ¾" below knot.

ZEBRA INSTRUCTIONS

SIDE OF BODY (make 2)

Begin at back leg. With size 3.50 mm hook and col A, ch 23.

Foundation row: 1 sc in second ch from hook, 1 sc in each ch to end, turn—22 sc.

Row 2: ch 3, 1 sc in second ch from hook, 1 sc in next ch, 1 sc in each sc to end, turn—24 sc.

Change to col B. Work throughout in stripes of 2 rows col B, 2 rows col A. Carry the yarns up the side edge of the work except where instructed to fasten off. For a neat finish, when changing cols, work the last pull through of a row in the col required for next row.

Row 3: ch 1, 1 sc in each sc to last sc, 2 sc in last sc, turn—25 sc.

Row 4: ch 3, 1 sc in second ch from hook, 1 sc in next ch, 1 sc in each of next 24 sc, 2 sc in last sc, turn—28 sc.

Row 5: work as for row 3—29 sc.

Row 6: ch 1, 2 sc in first sc, 1 sc in each sc to end, turn—30 sc.

Row 7: ch 1, 2 sc in first sc, 1 sc in each sc to last sc, 2 sc in last sc, turn—32 sc.

Row 8: ch 1, 1 sc in first sc, 1 sc in each sc to end, turn.

Row 9: work as for row 3—33 sc.

Row 10: work as for row 8. Fasten off both cols.

Back Leg Shaping

Row 11: Leave first 11 sc, rejoin col B to next sc, ch 1, 1 sc in next sc, 1 sc in each sc to last sc, 2 sc in last sc, turn—22 sc.

Row 12: ch 1, 1 sc in first sc, 1 sc in each sc to last 2 sc, sc2tog over last 2 sc, turn—21 sts.

Row 13: ch 1, sc2tog over first 2 sc, 1 sc in each sc to end, turn—20 sts.

Rows 14–24: work as for row 8. Fasten off col B.

Front Leg

Row 25: with col A, ch 15, 1 sc in second ch from hook, 1 sc in each of next 13 ch, 1 sc in each sc to end, turn—34 sc.

Row 26: work as for row 8.

Row 27: with col B, ch 1, 1 sc in first sc, 1 sc in each sc to last 2 sc, sc2tog over last 2 sc, turn—33 sts.

Row 28: ch 1, 1 sc in sc2tog, 1 sc in each sc to last sc, 2 sc in last sc, turn—34 sts.

Rows 29 and 30: work as for row 8.

Rows 31–34: work as for rows 27–30—34 sts. Fasten off col B.

Front Leg Shaping

Row 35: with col A, ch 1, 1 sc in each of first 7 sc, 1 sl st in next sc. Fasten off. Skip next 7 sc, rejoin col B to next sc, ch 1, 1 sc in each of next 17 sc to last sc, 2 sc in last sc, turn.

Row 36: ch 1, 2 sc in first sc, 1 sc in each sc to last 3 sc, sc2tog over next 2 sc, turn—18 sts.

Row 37: with col A, ch 1, sc2tog over first 2 sts, 1 sc in each sc to last sc, turn—18 sts.

Rows 38 and 39: work as for rows 36 and 37—17 sts.

Row 40: work as for row 36—16 sts.

Head Shaping

Row 41: ch 1, 2 sc in first sc, 1 sc in each sc to end, turn—17 sc.

Row 42: ch 1, 1 sc in first sc, 1 sc in each sc to last sc, 2 sc in last sc, turn—18 sc.

Row 43: ch 1, 2 sc in first sc, 1 sc in each sc to last sc, 2 sc in last sc, turn—20 sc.

Row 44: work as for row 42—21 sc.

Rows 45 and 46: work as for rows 41 and 42—23 sc.

Row 47: ch 1, 1 sc in first sc, 1 sc in each sc to last 2 sc, sc2tog over last 2 sc, turn—22 sts.

Row 48: work as for row 8.

Row 49: ch 1, sc2tog over first 2 sc, 1 sc in each sc to last 2 sc, sc2tog over last 2 sc, turn—20 sts.

Nose Shaping

Row 50: ch 1, sc2tog over first 2 sc, 1 sc in each of next 8 sc, 1 sl st in next sc, turn, leaving 9 sts unworked, ch 1, skip 1 sl st, 1 sc in each of next 7 sc, sc2tog over next 2 sts, turn, ch 1, sc2tog over first 2 sts, 1 sc in each of next 6 sc, 1 sl st in ch 1, 1 sc in each sc to last 2 sc, sc2tog over last 2 sc. Fasten off.

HEAD GUSSET

With size 3.50 mm hook and col B, ch 3.

Row 1: 1 sc in second ch from hook, 1 sc in next ch, turn—2 sc.

Row 2: ch 1, 1 sc in first sc, 1 sc in last sc, turn.

Change to col A. Work in stripes as for back.

Row 3: ch 1, 2 sc in first sc, 2 sc in last sc, turn—4 sc.

Row 4: ch 1, 1 sc in first sc, 1 sc in each sc to end, turn.

Row 5: ch 1, 2 sc in first sc, 1 sc in each sc to last sc, 2 sc in last sc, turn—6 sc.

Rows 6–8: work as for row 4.

Row 9: work as for row 5—8 sc.

Rows 10–14: work as for row 4.

Row 15: ch 1, sc2tog over first 2 sc, 1 sc in each sc to last 2 sc, sc2tog over last 2 sc, turn—6 sts.

Row 16: ch 1, 1 sc in sc2tog, 1 sc in each sc, ending 1 sc in sc2tog, turn.

Rows 17 and 18: work as for rows 15 and 16—4 sts.

Row 19: ch 1, sc2tog over first 2 sc, sc2tog over last 2 sc, turn—2 sts.

Row 20: ch 1, [1 sc in sc2tog] twice. Fasten off.

UNDERBODY

With size 3.50 mm hook and col B, ch 3. Work in col B throughout.

Row 1: 1 sc in second ch from hook, 1 sc in next ch, turn—2 sc.

Row 2: ch 1, 1 sc in each of next 2 sc, turn.

Row 3: ch 1, 2 sc in first sc, 1 sc in last sc, turn—3 sc.

Row 4: ch 1, 2 sc in first sc, 1 sc in each sc to end, turn—4 sc.

Rows 5–8: work as for row 4—8 sc.

Back Legs

Row 9: ch 15, 1 sc in second ch from hook, 1 sc in each of next 13 ch, 1 sc in each sc to end, turn—22 sc.

Row 10: work as for row 9—36 sc.

Row 11: ch 1, 1 sc in first sc, 1 sc in each sc to end, turn.

Row 12: work as for row 11.

Row 13: ch 1, 2 sc in first sc, 1 sc in each sc to end, turn—37 sc.

Row 14: work as for row 13—38 sc.

Rows 15–21: work as for row 11.

Back Leg Shaping

Row 22: ch 1, 1 sc in first sc, 1 sc in each of next 26 sc, turn, leaving 11 sc unworked.

Row 23: ch 1, 1 sc in first sc, 1 sc in each of next 15 sc, turn, leaving 11 sc unworked—16 sc.

Row 24: ch 1, sc2tog over first 2 sc, 1 sc in each sc to end, turn—15 sc.

Rows 25–31: work as for row 24—8 sc.

Rows 32–36: work as for row 11.

Front Legs

Rows 37–48: work as for rows 9–20—38 sc.

Row 49: ch 1, 1 sc in first sc, 1 sc in each of next 6 sc, 1 sl st in next sc, fasten off. Leave next 5 sc, rejoin yarn to next sc, ch 1, 1 sc in next sc, 1 sc in each sc to end—24 sc.

Row 50: work as for row 49—10 sc.

Rows 51 and 52: work as for row 11.

Row 53: ch 1, sc2tog over first 2 sc, 1 sc in each sc to end, turn—9 sc.

Row 54: work as for row 53—8 sts.

Rep rows 51–54 a total of 3 more times—2 sts.

Next row: ch 1, 1 sc in each of 2 sc, turn.

Foll row: ch 1, sc2tog over 2 rem sts. Fasten off.

EARS (make 2)

With size 3.50 mm hook and col A, ch 7.

Row 1: 1 sc in second ch from hook, 1 sc in each ch to end, turn—6 sc.

Row 2: ch 1, 1 sc in first sc, 1 sc in each sc to end, turn.

Rows 3–5: work as for row 2.

Row 6: ch 1, 1 sc in each of first 2 sc, sc2tog over next 2 sc, 1 sc in each of last 2 sc, turn—5 sts.

Row 7: ch 1, 1 sc in first sc, sc3tog over next 3 sts, 1 sc in last sc, turn—3 sts.

Row 8: ch 1, sc3tog over 3 rem sts. Fasten off.

MANE

Special Abbreviation: lp st loop st, worked as follows: insert hook as directed, hold yarn in a lp over left forefinger, catch both threads below finger at base of lp and pull through, yo, pull through 3 lps on hook, release the lp. The length of each lp is controlled by the forefinger.

With size 3.50 mm hook and col A, ch 31.
Row 1: 1 lp st in second ch from hook, 1 lp st in each ch to last ch, 2 lp st in last ch, turn and work back along base of ch: 1 lp st in base of each ch to end. Fasten off.

FINISHING

Join pieces and insert polyester stuffing as described for giraffe. Sew mane along center back seam, beginning at top of head and ending at center back.. Pull gently on each loop to tighten it, and then cut through and trim all the ends evenly to about ½".

Eyes

With size 3.50 mm hook and col C, ch 3 and join into a ring with 1 sl st in first ch made, (work over starting end) 6 sc into ring. Fasten off. Pull gently on starting end to tighten center. Sew one eye to each side of head, then with col A, stitch between eyes and work French knots as described for giraffe.

Tail

With col A, work tail as for giraffe.

RABBIT CURTAIN

TRY THE TRADITIONAL TECHNIQUE OF FILET CROCHET WORKED FROM A CHART TO MAKE A PRETTY WINDOW TREATMENT FOR THE NURSERY.

SIZE

Finished panel measures approximately 23½" x 33½", excluding hanging loops. For a longer curtain, work extra mesh pattern rows at the top, as required; for a wider curtain, work two or more panels.

MATERIALS

3 balls of Twilleys Lyscordet 4-ply (100% cotton, 100g), col 78 White *or* comparable yarn
2.00 mm and 2.50 mm hooks

GAUGE

14½ mesh squares and 11½ rows = 4" in mesh pattern with size 2.50 mm hook

PANEL

With size 2.50 mm hook, ch 169.
Chart row 1 (foundation row): 1 dc in fifth ch from hook, *ch 1, skip 1 ch, 1 dc in next ch, rep from * to end, turn. 83 mesh squares, as shown on row 1 of chart.
Chart row 2: ch 2, then read second row of chart from left to right: each blank square on the chart represents one mesh square, worked as [ch 1, skip 1 ch, 1 dc in next dc]; each filled square on the chart represents one block, worked as [1 dc in ch-1 sp, 1 dc in next dc], work last dc in third ch of ch 4 at beg row 1, turn.
Chart row 3: ch 2, then read third row of chart from right to left, in mesh pattern and blocks as before; where a mesh is worked above a block, work [ch 1, skip 1 dc, 1 dc in next dc] and where a block is worked above a block, work [1 dc in each of next 2 dc], work last dc in second ch of ch 3 at beg previous row, turn.

NOTE

Diagonal lines (for rabbit's whiskers and bird's beak) will be embroidered later. Cont reading from successive chart rows until chart row 94 is complete, or to length required.

BORDER

Change to size 2.00 mm hook.
Round 1: ch 2, 1 sc in first dc, *1 sc in ch-1 sp, 1 sc in next dc, rep from * to corner, ending [1 sc, ch 1, 1 sc] in second ch of ch 3; work 2 sc in side edge of each row to next corner, [1 sc, ch 1, 1 sc] in base of first ch, *1 sc in ch-1 sp, 1 sc in base of next ch, rep from * along lower edge to corner, ending [1dc, ch 1, 1dc] in second ch of ch 3 at corner; 2 sc in side edge of each row, ending 1 sl st in ch-2 sp at beg of round.
Round 2: ch 2, 1 sc in ch-2 sp at corner, *1 sc in each sc to corner,

[1 sc, ch 1, 1 sc] in ch-1 sp at corner, rep from *, ending 1 sl st in ch-2 sp at beg of round.
Rep round 2 twice more.

FIRST STRAP

Row 1: ch 1, 1 sc in ch-2 sp at corner, 1 sc in each of next 6 sc, turn.
***Row 2:** ch 1, 1 sc in each of next 7 sc, turn.
Rep this row until strap measures 3" or length required to fit curtain pole. Fasten off.

SECOND STRAP

With RS facing, skip next 14 sc, rejoin yarn to next sc, work as for first strap from * to end.
Make 7 more straps in this way along top edge. Note that on first row of last strap, last sc should be worked into ch-2 sp at corner.

EDGING

With RS facing and size 2.00 mm hook, join yarn to last sc of border at top right-hand corner of curtain, ch 1, *1 sc in side edge of each row of strap to corner, ch 1, fold strap toward wrong side of curtain, matching top edge to last row of border, [1 sc in next sc through both thicknesses] 7 times to next corner of strap, ch 1, 1 sc in side edge of each row down to last row of border, ending sc2tog at corner; 1 sc in each of 14 sc along last row of border, ending sc2tog at base of next strap, rep from * along top edge of work, ending 1 sl st in ch-1 sp at corner of border. Fasten off.
Embroider rabbit's whiskers and bird's beak as straight stitches.
Press as instructed on yarn labels.

MESH PATTERN

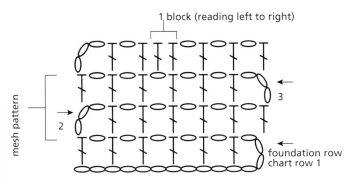

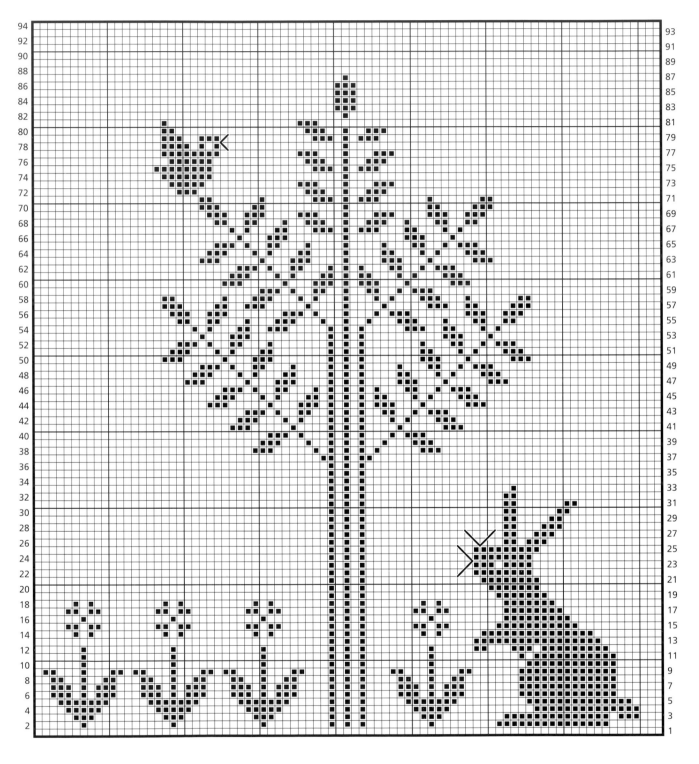

This design is completely reversible and looks good whichever way you decide to hang it. The reverse of the curtain is shown on page 101.

HEXAGON BLANKET

WARM AND LIGHT, THIS SNUG DESIGN CAN EASILY BE ADAPTED TO ANY SIZE REQUIRED.

SIZE

25" x 30½"

For a larger blanket, simply work more and/or longer strips. Note that extra yarn will be required: approx.1 ball of A for every 17 extra hexagons, and 1 ball of B for every 7 extra hexagons.

MATERIALS

2 balls of Fairytale DK by Patons (50g), col A (6302 Vanilla) *or* comparable yarn
5 balls of Fairytale DK Patons, col B (6304 Peppermint) *or* comparable yarn
3.50 mm and 4.00 mm hooks

GAUGE

First hexagon made should measure 5¼" from corner to opposite corner. If your hexagon is too small, try again with a larger hook; if it is too large, try a smaller hook. Gauge is not crucial provided a change in size is acceptable. However, if your gauge is too loose, extra yarn may be required.

Special Abbreviation: 1 rsc working from left to right (if you are right handed): insert hook into next sc to right with hook facing slightly downward, catch yarn and pull through, turning hook slightly back to the normal position; yo, pull through 2 lps on hook.

INSTRUCTIONS

STRIP A (make 4)
First Hexagon
With size 4.00 mm hook and col A, ch 3 and join into a ring with 1 sl st in first ch made.
Round 1: working over starting end: 6 sc into ring, 1 sl st into first sc.
Round 2: ch 3, tr2tog inserting hook in front lp only at base of these 3 ch (first petal made), *ch 4, tr3tog, inserting hook in front lp only of next sc (second petal made), rep from * 4 more times, ch 4, fasten off with 1 sl st in top of first petal. 6 petals made. Break off col A.
Round 3: join col B to back lp of sc behind first petal, ch 4, 3 tr in same place, 4 tr in back lp of next 5 sc, 1 sl st in fourth ch of ch 4 at beg of round.

HEXAGON PATTERN

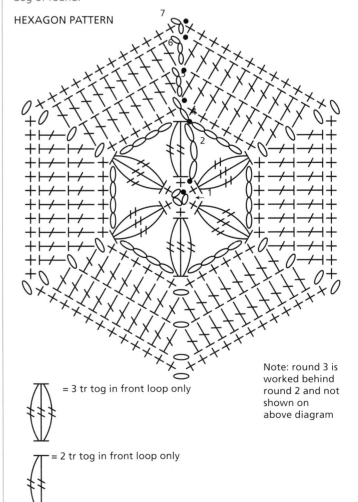

Note: round 3 is worked behind round 2 and not shown on above diagram

= 3 tr tog in front loop only

= 2 tr tog in front loop only

Round 4: 1 sl st in top of first petal, ch 2, 1 sc in same place as 1 sl st, *[1 sc in ch-4 sp tog with next tr behind] 4 times, [1 sc, ch 1, 1 sc] in top of next petal, rep from *, ending 1 sl st in ch-2 sp at beg of round.

Round 5: ch 3, 1 dc in ch-2 sp at base of these 3 ch, *1 dc in each of next 6 sc, [1 dc, ch 1, 1 dc] in ch-1 sp, rep from *, ending 1 dc in each of 6 sc, sl st in ch-3 sp at beg of round.

Round 6: ch 3, 1 dc in ch-3 sp at base of these 3 ch, *1 dc in each of next 8 dc, [1 dc, ch 1, 1 dc] in ch-1 sp, rep from *, ending join in col A, 1 sl st in ch-3 sp at beg of round. Break off col B.

Round 7: cont in col A: ch 2, 1 sc in ch-3 sp at base of these 2 ch, *1 sc in each of next 10 dc, [1 sc, ch 1, 1 sc] in ch-1 sp, rep from *, ending 1 sl st in first ch of ch 2 at beg of round. Fasten off. Pull gently on starting end of yarn to tighten center.

Second Hexagon
Work as for first hexagon without fastening off. Join to first hexagon as follows:

Place 2 hexagons side by side with RS up and second hexagon closest to you. Insert hook in next ch-1 sp of closest hexagon and out through corresponding ch-1 sp of hexagon above from back to front, yo, pull lp through both ch sps and lp on hook (1 sl st made). [Insert hook in back lp of next sc of closest hexagon and out through back lp of next sc of hexagon above from back to front, yo, pull lp through both sts and lp on hook (1 sl st made)] 12 times. Work 1 sl st, joining next 2 corresponding ch sps. Fasten off.

Work 3 more hexagons in the same way, joining them to form a strip of 5 as shown in diagram 1.

STRIP B (make 3)
Half Hexagon
With size 4.00 mm hook and col A, ch 3 and join into a ring with 1 sl st in first ch made.

Row 1: ch 1, 4 sc into ring, turn.

Row 2: ch 3, [yo twice, insert hook in front lp of sc at base of these 3 ch, yo, pull through a lp, (yo, pull through 2 lps) twice] twice in same place, yo, pull through 3 lps on hook (first petal made), *ch 4, tr3tog, inserting hook in front lp only of next sc (second petal made), rep from * twice more. (4 petals made.) Fasten off and turn the work.

Row 3: with WS facing, join col B to front lp of sc at base of last petal made, ch 4, 2 tr in same place, 4 tr in front lp of each of next 2 sc, 3 tr in front lp of next sc, turn.

Row 4: ch 1, 2 sc in top of first petal, skip first tr, *[1 sc in ch-4 sp tog with next tr behind] 4 times, [1 sc, ch 1, 1 sc] in top of next petal, rep from * once more, [1 sc in ch-4 sp tog with next tr behind] 4 times, 1 sc in top of last petal, 1 sc in same place tog with fourth ch of ch 4 at beg of previous row, turn.

Row 5: ch 3, 1 dc in first sc, *1 dc in each of next 6 sc, [1 dc, ch 1, 1 dc] in ch-1 sp, rep from * once more, 1 dc in each of next 6 sc, 2 dc in last sc, turn.

Row 6: ch 3, 1 dc in first dc, *1 dc in each of next 8 dc, [1 dc, ch 1, 1 dc] in ch-1 sp, rep from * once more, 1 dc in each of next 8 dc, 2 dc in third ch of ch 3 at beg of previous row. Fasten off.

Row 7: with RS facing, join col A to third ch of ch 3 at beg row 6, ch 2, 1 sc in same place as base of ch 2, [1 sc in each of next 10 dc, (1 sc, ch 1, 1 sc) in ch-1 sp] twice, 1 sc in each of next 10 dc, [1 sc, ch 1, 1 sc] in last dc. Fasten off.

See diagram 2. Work 4 whole hexagons (as second hexagon of strip A) and another half hexagon, joining them as shown.

Join the strips as shown in diagram 3:
Place 2 strips side by side with right sides up. Join col A to ch-1 sp of

closest strip at right-hand side of seam. Insert hook in same ch sp and out through corresponding ch-1 sp of strip above from WS to RS, yo, pull lp through both ch sps and lp on hook (1 sl st made). *[Insert hook in back lp of next sc of closest strip and out through corresponding lp above from back to front of motif, yo, pull lp through both stitches and lp on hook (1 sl st made)] 12 times. Work 1 sl st, joining next seam with corresponding ch sp. Rep from * all along the seam. Fasten off.

BORDER
Round 1: With RS facing and size 3.50 mm hook, join col A to ch-1 sp at one corner of blanket, ch 2, 1 sc in same ch-1 sp, work all around in sc as follows: along short sides, work 1 sc in each sc, sc2tog at each inner corner and [1 sc, ch 1, 1 sc] in ch-1 sp at each outer point; along long sides, work 1 sc in each sc and ch sp of hexagons, and work 21 sc along side edge of each half hexagon (including 3 sc worked into center ring). End round with 1 sl st in ch-2 sp at beg of round.

Round 2: ch 1, 1 sc in each sc of previous round, working sc2tog at inner corners and 2 sc in each ch-1 sp at outer points, ending 1 sl st under ch 1 at beg of round.

Round 3: Without turning, work reverse sc from left to right (if you are right handed): ch 1, 1 rsc in each sc all around, skipping 1 sc at each inner corner, ending 1 sl st under ch 1 at beg of round. Fasten off.

Press as instructed on yarn labels.

diagram 3

diagram 1 (strip A)

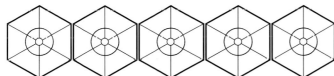

diagram 2 (strip B)

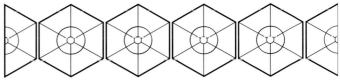

NURSERY PILLOW

THIS PILLOW IS MADE WITH SIMPLE SQUARES OF DOUBLE CROCHET
AND BOLD APPLIQUÉ SHAPES, WHICH ARE TRIMMED WITH EASY
CHAIN-STITCH EMBROIDERY.

SIZE

to fit pillow form   18" x 18"

MATERIALS

2 balls of Tropicana DK by Sirdar (100% acrylic,
100g/262yds), col A (728 Watersprite) *or* comparable yarn
1 ball of Tropicana DK by Sirdar, col B (710 White) *or*
comparable yarn
1 ball of Tropicana DK by Sirdar, col C (713 Dune) *or*
comparable yarn
3.50 mm hook
14"-long zipper
Blunt-ended tapestry needle and Darning needle
Thin cardstock

GAUGE

18 sts and 9 rows = 4" in rows of double crochet pattern
with size 3.50 mm hook. Gauge is not crucial provided a
change in size is acceptable; however, if your gauge is too
loose, extra yarn may be required.

RABBIT MOTIF

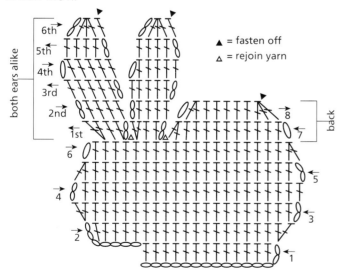

INSTRUCTIONS FOR FRONT

RABBIT SQUARE (make 2)

With size 3.50 mm hook and col A, ch 35.

Foundation row (RS row): 1 dc in third ch from hook, 1 dc in each ch to end, turn—34 sts.

Row 1 (WS row): ch 2, skip first dc, 1 dc in each dc, ending 1 dc in second ch of ch 2, turn.

Rep this row 16 more times—18 rows in all. Fasten off.

Rabbit (make 2)

With size 3.50 mm hook and col B, ch 15.

Row 1: 1 dc in third ch from hook, 1 dc in each ch to end, turn—14 sts.

Row 2: 7 ch, 1 dc in third ch from hook, 1 dc in each of next 4 ch, 1 dc in each dc, ending 2 dc in second ch of ch 2, turn—21 sts.

Row 3: ch 2, 1 dc in first dc, 1 dc in each dc, ending 2 dc in second ch of ch 2, turn—23 sts.

Row 4: ch 2, skip first dc, 1 dc in each dc, ending 1 dc in second ch of ch 2, turn.

Row 5: ch 2, skip first dc, 1 dc in each dc to last dc and ch 2, dc2tog over last 2 sts, turn—22 sts.

Row 6: ch 1, skip dc2tog, 1 dc in each dc to last dc and ch 2, dc2tog over last 2 sts—21 sts.

Row 7: ch 1, skip dc2tog, 1 dc in each of next 10 dc, dc2tog over next 2 dc, turn and complete back of rabbit as follows:

diagram 1   diagram 2

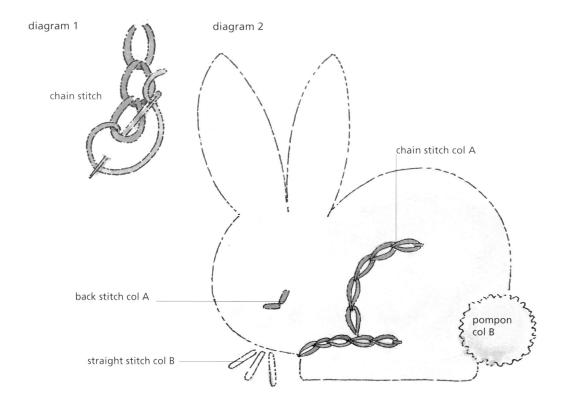

chain stitch

chain stitch col A

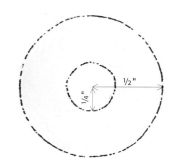

back stitch col A

straight stitch col B

pompon col B

Row 8: ch 1, skip dc2tog, dc2tog over next 2 dc, 1 dc in each of next 5 dc, dc3tog over last 3 dc. Fasten off.

First Ear
Rejoin yarn to next dc at end of row 7.
Row 1: ch 2, 1 dc in dc at base of these 2 ch, 1 dc in next dc, 2 dc in next dc, turn—5 sts.
Row 2: ch 2, skip first dc, 1 dc in each of next 3 dc, 1 dc in second of ch 2, turn.
Row 3: ch 2, 1 dc in dc at base of these 2 ch, 1 dc in each of next 3 dc, 1 dc in second ch of ch 2, turn—6 sts.
Row 4: ch 1, skip first dc, 1 dc in each of next 4 dc, 1 dc in second ch of ch 2, turn.
Row 5: ch 2, skip first dc, 1 dc in each of next 4 dc, turn—5 sts.
Row 6: ch 2, skip first dc, dc3tog over next 3 dc, 1 dc in second ch of ch 2. Fasten off.

Second Ear
Rejoin yarn to next dc at end of row 1 of first ear.
Work rows 1–6 as for first ear.
With RS of rabbit squares facing, sew 1 rabbit to each square, facing in opposite directions as shown in photograph. With a blunt-ended tapestry needle and col B, work in back stitch around the edge of the motif without splitting the yarn. With col A, embroider outline of leg in chain stitch and closed eye in back stitch. With col B, embroider lines for whiskers in straight stitch.
(See diagrams 1 and 2.)

Tail (make 2)
Cut 2 circles of cardstock as shown in diagram 3. Place them together and wind with col B as in diagram 4 until central hole is full. Insert point of scissors between the card layers and cut through strands all around edge. Tie a length of yarn firmly around the center between the card circles, then snip away the card.
Sew 1 pompon tail to each rabbit.

diagram 3

½"
¼"

diagram 4

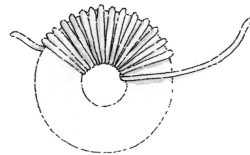

FLOWER SQUARE (make 2)

With col B, work as for rabbit square.

Flower (make 6)

Round 1: with size 3.50 mm hook and col C, ch 4 and join into a ring with 1 sl st in first ch made.

Round 2: ch 1, 8 sc into ring, 1 sl st into first sc of round—8 sts.

Round 3: ch 3, 1 dc in sc at base of these 3 ch, *ch 1, [1 dc, ch 1, 1 dc] in next sc, rep from *, ending ch 1, 1 sl st in second ch of ch 3 at beg of round. Fasten off.

Leaf (make 12)

With size 3.50 mm hook and col A, ch 3.

Row 1: 2 dc in third ch from hook, turn—3 sts.

Row 2: ch 2, skip first dc, 3 dc in next dc, 1 dc in second of ch 2, turn—5 sts.

Row 3: ch 2, skip first dc, 1 dc in each of 3 dc, 1 dc in second of ch 2, turn.

Row 4: ch 1, skip first dc, dc3tog over next 3 dc, 1 dc in second ch of ch 2. Fasten off.

With RS of flower squares facing, arrange 3 flowers on each flower square and sew in place as before. With col A, work a stem in chain stitch for each flower. Sew 6 leaves to each square in pairs as shown.

Arrange squares as shown in diagram 5. Hold the top 2 squares with WS facing and use 3.50 mm hook to join col C to top corner of right hand square, ch 1, 1 sc in side edge of last row of left-hand square, 1 sc in next-to-last row of right-hand square, *1 sc in next

FLOWER

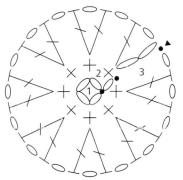

LEAF

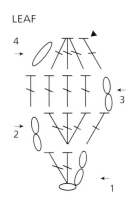

diagram 5 (front)

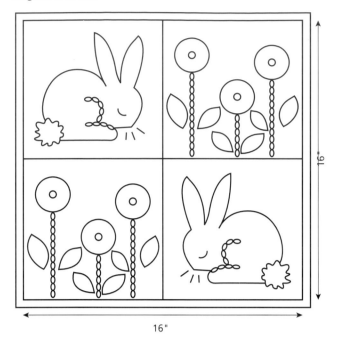

16"

16"

diagram 6 (back)

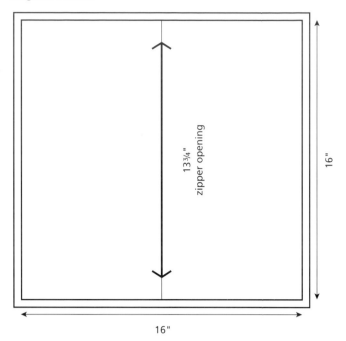

13¾"
zipper opening

16"

16"

row of left hand square, 1 sc in next row of right hand square, rep from *, ending 1 sl st in lower corner of right-hand square. Fasten off. Join the other 2 squares in the same way. Then join the 2 strips as follows: Place the 2 strips with WS facing. With size 3.50 mm hook, join col C to top of last dc at right-hand corner of lower strip, ch 1, 1 sc in sp between first and second sts of upper strip, *skip 1 dc on lower strip, 1 sc in next dc, skip 2 dc on upper strip, 1 sc in next sp, rep from * all across, ending 1 sl st in last dc of lower strip. Fasten off.

INSTRUCTIONS FOR BACK

BACK PANEL (make 2)
With size 3.50 mm hook, and col A, ch 35.
Foundation row: 1 dc in third ch from hook, 1 dc in each ch to end, turn—34 sts.
Row 1: ch 2, skip first dc, 1 dc in each dc, ending 1 dc in second ch of ch 2, turn.
Rep this row 34 more times—36 rows in all. Fasten off.
Place the 2 panels with WS together and join for about 1" at each end of seam, leaving a 14" opening for zipper as shown in diagram 6.
Work around zipper opening as follows: with RS facing and size 3.50 mm hook, join col A to seam at one end of opening, ch 1, 2 sc in side edge of each row to other end of opening, sc2tog at corner, 2 sc in side edge of each row down to first end, ending 1 sc tog with 1 sl st in first sc made. Fasten off.
Baste the opening closed, matching row ends. Pin closed zipper to wrong side of opening. Tack in place. With col A and darning needle, backstitch all around zipper, just inside crochet edge. Remove basting.

INSTRUCTIONS FOR BORDERS

BACK
With RS of back facing and size 3.50 mm hook, join col C to last dc at top right-hand corner.
Round 1: ch 3, 1 sc in dc at base of these 3 ch, 1 sc in each of next 33 sts, 1 sc in seam, 1 sc in each of next 34 sts to corner (69 sc along top edge), ch 2, 2 sc in side edge of each row to corner (72 sc along second side), ch 2, 1 sc in base of each of 34 sts, 1 sc in seam, 1 sc in base of each of 34 sts (69 sc along lower edge), ch 2, 2 sc in side edge of each of next 35 rows, 1 sc in side edge of next row, 1 sl st in first ch of ch 3 (72 sts along fourth side).
Round 2: ch 3, 1 sc in ch-3 lp, work in sc along top edge, working [2 sc in 1 sc] 3 times evenly spaced; at corner, work [1 sc, ch 2, 1 sc] in ch-2 sp; 1 sc in each sc down second side, ending [1 sc, ch 2, 1 sc] in ch-2 sp at corner; work along lower edge in same way as top edge, ending [1 sc, ch 2, 1 sc] in ch-2 sp at corner; 1 sc in each sc up fourth side, ending 1 sl st in first ch of ch 3—74 sts along each side. Fasten off.

FRONT
Cut three 4-yard lengths of col C and set aside.
Using main ball of col C, work as for back border without fastening off.
Place front and back with WS together.
Next round: work through both thicknesses all around: ch 3, 1 sc in both ch-2 sps, *1 sc in each sc to corner, [1 sc, ch 2, 1 sc] in both ch-2 sps, rep from *, ending 1 sl st in first ch of ch 3.
Edging round: double the 3 lengths of col C and work 1 sc into 3 lps of yarn thus formed tog with next ch-2 sp, then complete the round working over the 6 yarn ends, pulling them gently every few sts for an even finish: 2 sc in same ch-2 sp, *1 sc in each sc to corner, 3 sc in ch-2 sp, rep from *, ending 1 sl st in first sc of round. Fasten off. Trim the yarn ends to different lengths and run them in under the first few sts of last round to make a smooth join.
Press as instructed on yarn labels.
Insert pillow form.

RESOURCES

For a list of shops in your area that carry the yarns mentioned in this book, write to the following companies.

For Sirdar Yarns
Distributed by
Knitting Fever
35 Debevoise Ave.
Roosevelt, NY 11575
516-546-3600
Web: www.knittingfever.com

For Wendy Yarns
Distributed by
Berroco, Inc.
14 Elmdale Rd.
Uxbridge, MA 01569
508-278-2527
Web: www.berroco.com

For Jaegar Yarns
Distributed by
Westminster Fibers
5 Northern Blvd Ste 3,
Amherst, NH 03031-2335
603-886-5041

For 2-ply Silk Yarn (ref. SS16)
Distributed by
Texere Yarns
College Mill
Barkerend Road
Bradford
BD1 4AU
E-mail: enquiries@texere-yarns.co.uk
Web: www.texere-yarns.co.uk

For Twilleys Lyscordet
Twilleys of Stamford
Roman Mill
Stamford
PE9 1BS
Web: www.tbramsden.co.uk

ACKNOWLEDGMENTS
Special thanks to Sue Whiting.